OTTAWA TRAVEL GUIDE 2023, CANADA

D1529003

Unveiling Ottawa, A Journey of Timeless Charms and Unforgettable Discoveries.

Jack C. Parish

TABLE OF CONTENT

INTRODUCTION

Welcome to Ottawa

The charming city of Ottawa, which is nestled on the gorgeous banks of the Ottawa River, provides a warm and sincere welcome to all those looking for an outstanding experience in Canada's capital. You will be welcomed with a feeling of history, adventure, and culture as soon as you set foot in this dynamic city, promising a thrilling voyage that will leave an enduring impression on your heart.

The city of Ottawa, which is proud of its extensive history, serves as a living example of both the past and present of Canada. Historic sites and architectural wonders may be found around every turn, beckoning you to travel through time. The distinctive emblem of the country's government is Parliament Hill, with its magnificent Gothic Revival structures, where you may see the political pulse of the nation against a background of magnificence. The perfume of delicious foods and the bustle of active conversations will tantalise your senses as you explore the historic ByWard Market, the longest continuously functioning market in Canada, and transport you to a bygone period.

The cultural fabric of Ottawa is fascinating and varied. While the Canadian Museum of History tells the interesting tales of the country's history via compelling displays, art fans can find refuge in the National Gallery of Canada, which has an excellent collection of Canadian and international art. The Canadian Museum of Indigenous History, which provides significant insights into the rich traditions and wisdom of Canada's First Nations, demonstrates the city's strong devotion to its Indigenous legacy.

Ottawa's natural beauty serves as a playground of thrills and excitement for those who seek adventure. Gatineau Park, a vast wilderness at a short distance from the city, provides a wide range of outdoor pursuits, such as trekking through rocky trails and taking in the stunning views from the Eardley Escarpment. The Rideau Canal becomes the biggest skating rink in the world during the winter, making for a wonderful experience as you skate beneath the stars.

As dusk falls, Ottawa's exciting nightlife begins to take shape, entrancing your senses with its vivacious energy and entertainment options. The city's nightlife offers something for everyone, from little bars where local musicians serenade you with soulful tunes to stylish cocktail clubs where mixologists create delectable concoctions.

The culinary culture in Ottawa is exciting in and of itself, delivering a delicious blend of tastes from all around the globe. Your taste senses are in for a treat whether you indulge in typical Canadian fare like poutine and butter tarts or explore the varied cuisines in the ethnic neighbourhoods.

Each of Ottawa's lovely neighbourhoods reveals more of its own personality as you explore them deeper. Each neighbourhood provides an entire experience and a window into the life of the residents, from the busy downtown with its striking skyline to the cultural hotspot of Little Italy and the bohemian atmosphere of Hintonburg.

Ottawa offers something to enthral everyone, regardless of whether you're travelling with family, friends, or alone. Families will appreciate the variety of family-friendly activities available, which range from parks and playgrounds that provide unlimited fun for young children to interactive museums and educational facilities.

A Brief History of Ottawa

The development of a thriving capital city and Indigenous heritage weave together throughout Ottawa's history to form a rich tapestry. Indigenous peoples, especially the Algonquin people, who have a strong connection to the land, used to live in the region where Ottawa is now.

As a focal site of struggle between the French and British colonial powers at the beginning of the 19th century, the area acquired prominence. To stop future American expansion, the British built a military outpost nearby in 1800. The community, which was once known as Bytown, came up around where the Rideau Canal, a vital canal connecting Lake Ontario and the Ottawa River, was being built. The canal was built under Lieutenant Colonel John By's supervision, and the city's development was significantly influenced by its completion in 1832.

The United Province of Canada, which subsequently changed its name to the Dominion of Canada in 1867, chose Ottawa as its capital in 1857 at the request of Queen Victoria. Ottawa was chosen as the nation's capital in part because of its advantageous position straddling the border between English- and French-speaking Canada, which symbolised the unification of the newly constituted country.

The creation of Ottawa as the capital resulted in a fast growth and expansion of the city. Grand government structures were built, adding to the city's stunning architectural panorama and includes the famed Parliament Hill. The Centre Block on Parliament Hill, with its noticeable Peace Tower, continues to be a well-known representation of the Canadian government.

Ottawa kept growing and prospering during the late 19th and early 20th centuries, and its population grew as well. As a significant administrative and military hub for Canada during both World Wars I and II, the city was essential.

Over time, Ottawa's social and cultural fabric become stronger. The city embraced its Native American past, recognising and honouring the First Nations peoples' contributions to Canadian identity and culture. In order to preserve and present the rich history and aesthetic accomplishments of the country, museums and galleries were founded.

As the federal government increased its presence in Ottawa in the second half of the 20th century, more people and companies moved there. As it grew, the city became a vibrant centre for politics, innovation, and diversity.

Today, Ottawa is a thriving, cutting-edge capital city where the past and present coexist together. It still serves as a hub of political power, hosting several government agencies and embassies in addition to fostering a vibrant tech and innovation industry.

Visitors discover a city that has accepted its history while embracing a promising future as they stroll around Ottawa's streets and neighbourhoods. Travellers from all over the globe are drawn to the city because of its distinctive fusion of history, culture, and unspoiled natural beauty, which makes it an alluring destination.

About the Travel Guide

The Ottawa Travel Guide is a comprehensive and painstakingly compiled resource created to be your ideal travel companion while you explore Ottawa, Canada's exciting capital city. This book includes a variety of useful information, insightful suggestions, and useful hints to make your trip an outstanding experience. It is designed to meet the requirements of both experienced travellers and first-time visitors.

The book offers a thorough and current overview of Ottawa's cultural history, natural marvels, adventure destinations, gastronomic pleasures, and dynamic entertainment scenes. It was written by a team of enthusiastic travel professionals and seasoned residents. It seeks to provide you a thorough grasp of the history, multiculturalism, and modern way of life of the city.

The Travel Guide starts out with a kind welcome, exposing you to Ottawa's attractions and tempting you to go off on a journey full of cultural discoveries, exciting adventures, and magical encounters. It takes pleasure in highlighting Ottawa's exceptional balancing act between maintaining its historical origins and embracing modernity, producing a harmonic combination that attracts a variety of tourists.

The user-friendly layout of the handbook includes a well-organised table of topics that makes it simple to move between its numerous parts. The guide makes sure you have rapid access to the material that matters most to you, whether you're looking for historical insights, suggestions for family-friendly activities, or advice on sustainable travel.

The goal of the book is to make your vacation experience better in every way. The book enables you to picture your adventure in Ottawa with colourful descriptions, engrossing storylines, and breathtaking photography, igniting your desire to discover its wealth of attractions.

The book emphasises responsible travel and eco-conscious behaviours in addition to offering a wealth of information on Ottawa's must-see sights, hidden treasures, and top-notch eating venues. It promotes sustainability, encourages patronising small businesses, and fosters a closer connection with the city's natural and cultural history.

The Ottawa Travel Guide has everything you need to make the most of your trip, whether your plans are to explore Ottawa's museums and galleries, stroll through its picturesque parks and rivers, savour its many culinary pleasures, or just take in the city's energetic vibe.

This book will be your trustworthy travel companion throughout the whole process, providing insights, ideas, and helpful suggestions to make sure your stay in Ottawa is nothing short of extraordinary. So embrace your inner explorer, follow your curiosity, and let the Ottawa Travel Guide guide you on a memorable journey into the heart of Canada's attractive capital city.

PLANNING YOUR TRIP TO OTTAWA

Packing Tips

It's important to combine readiness with practicality when packing for a vacation to Ottawa to make sure you have everything you need for a relaxing and pleasurable trip. To make the most of your trip to Canada's capital city, consider the following packing advice:

1. Dress for the weather: Ottawa has four different seasons, so it's important to prepare appropriately. Bring breathable, lightweight clothes like t-shirts, shorts, and sundresses as summers may be warm. Winters, on the other hand, may be chilly and snowy, so be sure to take layers of warm clothing like insulated jackets, sweaters, scarves, gloves, and a good pair of winter boots. As rain is frequent in the spring and autumn, don't forget to carry an umbrella or rainproof garment.

2. Comfy Shoes: Because Ottawa is a walking city with plenty of outdoor activities, it is important to have comfy shoes. For any potential outdoor trips as well as city exploration, bring along a pair of comfortable walking shoes or trainers.

3. Travel papers: Double-check that you have all appropriate travel papers, such as your passport, a visa (if applicable), and any other forms of identification or travel authorization. Keep these records in a location that is both safe and convenient.

4. Money and Payment Options: Although Ottawa accepts credit cards extensively, it's a good idea to have some Canadian money on hand in small quantities for modest purchases and transactions. To prevent any problems using your cards overseas, let your bank know about your vacation intentions.

5. Travel adaptor and charger: Be sure you include an adapter that works with Canadian power outlets. Also, remember to bring chargers for all of your electrical gadgets, including computers, cameras, and phones.

6. Personal Medications: Make sure you have enough of any prescription drugs you need to last the length of your trip if you use them. A modest first-aid kit filled with necessary items like bandages, painkillers, and any other over-the-counter prescriptions you may need should also be packed.

7. Wear sunglasses and sunscreen to shield yourself from the sun's rays, particularly during the summer. To protect your eyes from UV radiation, bring sunglasses and sunscreen with a high SPF.

8. Travel-Sized Toiletries: Choose travel-sized toiletries to save space and adhere to flight requirements. Bring any necessary personal hygiene goods, such as toothbrush, shampoo, and conditioner.

9. Reusable Water Bottle: Bring a reusable water bottle with you on your adventures to stay hydrated. There are several public water fountains in Ottawa where you may refill it.

10. Daypack or Backpack: While visiting the city, a modest daypack or backpack comes in helpful for transporting your necessities. Snacks, a water bottle, a camera, and any trinkets you pick up along the trip may also be carried in it.

11. Lightweight trip handbook: Even though there is a wealth of material accessible online, having a lightweight trip handbook on hand may be helpful for inspiration and rapid reference.

You'll be well-prepared to make the most of your stay in Ottawa by packing wisely and taking into account the particular weather and activities you'll be participating in. This way, you'll be able to create priceless memories and experiences in Canada's enchanting capital city.

Weather and Climate

There are four different seasons in Ottawa, and each one provides tourists with a unique and enthralling experience. You can prepare smartly and plan your activities by being aware of the weather and environment. Here is a summary of the weather and climate in Ottawa throughout the course of the year:

1. Spring (March to May): Ottawa comes to life in the spring as blossoming flowers and lush foliage fill the city.
   - The average temperature is between 3°C and 15°C (37°F and 59°F), however it may be fairly erratic, with frigid days and warm spurts sporadically occurring.
   - Dress in layers to adjust for temperature fluctuations. Bring light sweaters, long-sleeve shirts, and a medium-weight jacket. Because spring

showers are common, bring a rainproof jacket or umbrella.

2. Summer (June to August): Ottawa has sunny, pleasant summers that are full with outdoor festivals and festivities. Although temperatures seldom exceed 30°C (86°F), they typically vary from 15°C to 27°C (59°F to 81°F).
   - Pack t-shirts, shorts, skirts, and sandals, as well as other lightweight, breathable items. For sun protection, don't forget to pack sunscreen, a hat, and sunglasses.

3. Autumn (September to November): The changing of the leaves in Ottawa's autumn season results in breathtaking foliage and a gorgeous scene.
   - The typical temperature ranges from 45°F to 66°F (7°C to 19°C). Temperatures steadily lower as the year goes on. Pack a variety of warm-weather and cold-weather outfits. To keep comfortable during temperature changes, layering is key. Even though autumn might be a reasonably dry season, it's still a good idea to keep an umbrella or rainproof garment on hand.

4. Winter (December to February): Ottawa has chilly, snowy winters that provide a wide range of options for winter sports and activities.

- The average temperature is between -13°C and -6°C (9°F and 21°F), however it may become quite cold very quickly.

- Pack many layers of warm winter attire, such as insulated jackets, sweaters, scarves, gloves, thermal socks, and a cap. Walking on snowy and slippery areas requires sturdy winter boots with a strong grip.

- Make sure you bring the right equipment or rent it locally if you want to participate in winter activities like skiing or ice skating.

Overall, the weather and climate of Ottawa provide a variety of experiences all year round. Every season in Canada's capital city has its own special beauty and opportunity for unforgettable experiences, whether you're admiring the autumn foliage during the pleasant summers, seeing the city's museums and sites during the cool winters or taking part in winter sports in the snow.

Travel Insurance

Travel insurance is a crucial component of trip preparation that offers financial security and peace of mind while travelling. It provides protection against a variety of unanticipated occurrences that can interfere with or negatively affect your travel. Here are some reasons why having travel insurance is essential and what it usually covers:

1. Vacation Cancellation or Interruption: If you need to cancel or shorten your vacation for one of the covered reasons, such as sickness, injury, or unanticipated circumstances, travel insurance may pay you for non-refundable charges.

2. Medical Emergencies: Travel insurance may pay for medical costs, hospital stays, and even medical evacuations if required if you become sick or hurt while travelling.

3. Trip Delay or Missed Connection: Travel insurance may reimburse extra costs incurred as a result of delays or missed connections brought on by covered events like bad weather or airline strikes.

4. Baggage Loss or Delay: Travel insurance may cover the cost of replacing critical things in the event that your baggage is misplaced, stolen, or delayed by the airline.

5. Personal Liability: Travel insurance may provide defence against third-party lawsuits alleging that you were at fault for injuries or damage they sustained during a trip.

6. Emergency Evacuation: Travel insurance may pay for emergency evacuations to safeguard your safety in the event of a natural catastrophe, political turmoil, or other situations.

7. Pre-existing Medical disorders: If you satisfy certain criteria and buy the insurance within a specified amount of time after planning your trip, certain travel insurance plans cover pre-existing medical disorders.

Understand the coverage limitations, restrictions, and any extra alternatives you may need depending on your trip plans and personal circumstances before getting travel insurance. In order to guarantee that you have appropriate coverage, it's also crucial to correctly declare any pre-existing medical issues.

Various insurance companies, tour operators, and internet comparison websites all provide travel insurance. Prices vary according to the coverage, length of the trip, location, and the age and health of the traveller.

Although travel insurance is not required, it is strongly advised, particularly for foreign travel and holidays that would cost a lot of money. Purchasing travel insurance will protect you against possible financial losses and unanticipated crises, letting you concentrate on having a great time in Ottawa and making priceless memories without having to worry.

Transportation

In Ottawa, transport is quick, dependable, and provides a variety of routes for moving about the city and its environs. Ottawa features a transport system that may meet your requirements, whether you prefer utilising public transport, leasing a vehicle, or using ridesharing services. The primary forms of transit in Ottawa are as follows:

1. Public Transit (OC Transpo): OC Transpo, Ottawa's public transit provider, operates a vast bus network and the O-Train light rail system.
    - Buses run all around the city and link to different neighbourhoods, popular tourist destinations, and administrative offices.

- The O-Train Confederation Line is a quick and practical light rail service that connects Ottawa's east and west ends, passing through the city centre.

2. The O-Train Trillium Line:
   - A separate light rail route called the O-Train Trillium route runs from South Ottawa to downtown Ottawa and back. It connects Bayview Station in the heart of Ottawa with Greenboro Station in the south.

3. Ride-Share Services: Uber and Lyft are two examples of ride-share services that are available in Ottawa. These services provide a practical and accessible way to move about the city, particularly after hours or when public transport may not be as frequent.

4. Taxis: Ottawa offers conventional taxi services as well. You may either phone for a pickup or locate cabs at approved taxi stops.

5. riding: Ottawa is a bike-friendly city, and there are many riding trails and lanes all over the place. Consider hiring a bike from one of the city's bike-sharing programmes or a nearby rental store if you love riding.

6. Rental Cars: There are several automobile rental companies in Ottawa if you'd like the independence of having your own vehicle. Check parking choices before travelling since parking in downtown Ottawa may be scarce and expensive.

Walking is a fun and environmentally responsible method to see the city since many of Ottawa's attractions and neighbourhoods are accessible on foot.
 - The small downtown area of Ottawa makes it possible to stroll between the city's top attractions.

8. Via Rail and Greyhound: - Via Rail and Greyhound provide rail and bus services, respectively, to and from Ottawa to other Canadian cities.

Consider the distance between sites, the accessibility of public transportation, and the best mode of transportation depending on your itinerary and preferences when organising your transportation in Ottawa. While minimising your environmental impact, using a combination of public transportation, walking, and ride-share services may be an effective and affordable way to experience the city.

Currency and Exchange Rates

When visiting Ottawa and other regions of Canada, visitors must take currency and exchange rates into account. Here is a description of Canadian money along with some advice on managing your money while travelling:

Currency: The Canadian Dollar, represented by the currency codes CAD and $, is the official unit of exchange in Canada. The symbol represents one cent, the 100th smaller unit that makes up the Canadian Dollar.

There are many different denominations of banknotes in use, including $5, $10, $20, $50, and $100 bills with recognisable Canadian icons on them. Additionally, "loonies" and "toonies," two types of coins, are often used. The "toonie" is the two-dollar coin, which stands out for its two-toned design, while the "loonie" refers to the one-dollar coin, which has a common loon on the reverse side.

currency Rates: There are variations in currency rates among various exchange providers. To gain an idea of the worth of your money in Canadian Dollars before your travel, it is important to verify the current exchange rates. You may research exchange rates online, speak with your bank, or a trusted source of currency conversion.

Currency Exchange: Ottawa offers a broad range of currency exchange services, particularly in the downtown and other popular tourist areas. Currency exchange services are provided by banks, exchange bureaus, and certain hotels. To make sure you're getting the greatest bargain, it's a good idea to compare prices and charges.

ATMs: Automated teller machines, or ATMs, are commonly used in Ottawa and accept the majority of major credit cards as well as debit cards. Withdrawing Canadian Dollars from an ATM usually offers a cheap exchange rate and is convenient. To prevent any problems with your cards, however, be sure to ask your bank about international transaction fees and let them know about your vacation plans.

Credit Cards: The majority of hotels, restaurants, stores, and attractions in Ottawa accept credit cards, particularly Visa and Mastercard. For minor purchases or transactions at locations that may not take cards, it's always a good idea to have some cash on hand.

Traveler's Cheques: Although they were formerly a standard way to pay for travel, traveller's cheques are now less often utilised. Traveler's checks could not be widely accepted in Ottawa, so it's best to use credit cards, debit cards, or cash instead.

Overall, Ottawa is a cutting-edge city with a sound financial system, making it simple for tourists to handle their finances and transactions. It's a good idea to have a variety of payment methods, such as cash for convenience and cards for minor transactions. You may completely enjoy the city's charms, visit its sights, and savour its gastronomic pleasures without stress if you come prepared with Canadian Dollars.

Language and Communication

Ottawa is a bilingual city that reflects the distinct cultural identity of Canada by blending English and French in language and communication. Here is a list of the languages spoken in Ottawa along with some advice for communicating while you are there:

Languages Spoken:

1. English: The most common language in Ottawa is English. It is the primary language utilised in social interactions, commercial transactions, and official matters. The majority of individuals in Ottawa speak English well.

2. French: Ottawa is situated in the mostly English-speaking province of Ontario. Ottawa, the nation's capital, is nonetheless close to Quebec, a region where French is the official language. As a consequence, Ottawa has a large French-speaking population, particularly in the government, economic, and cultural sectors.

It is a fundamental component of Canadian identity because both English and French are recognised as official languages in Canada. English and French translations of several signs, official papers, and government services are provided. The federal government requires all workers to be bilingual or have access to multilingual services. The Canadian Parliament holds debates and official processes in both languages.

Communication Advice:
1. Greetings: You may just say "Hello" or "Bonjour" (which is French for "Hello"). Additionally, English

salutations such as "Hi" and "How are you?" are often used.

2. Politeness: Canadians have a reputation for being kind and polite. In every contact, using the words "please" and "thank you" is quite helpful.

3. Language Preference: Although the majority of Ottawa residents are multilingual and able to transition between English and French, it's polite to inquire about someone's preferred language before striking up a conversation, particularly if you are unsure of which language they may feel more at ease with.

4. Language Services: Don't worry if your French or English language skills aren't very strong. Many businesses, particularly those in the tourist industry, have multilingual staff members and language assistance services ready to help you.

5. Language Learning: If you're keen on picking up a few fundamental French expressions, it might be a pleasant and courteous method to get a feel for the community. The people there will value your attempts to communicate with them in their language.

Ottawa's bilingualism gives the city's culture and communication a distinctive edge. You'll find the residents to be kind and accommodating whether you know English, French, or both. If you embrace linguistic variety, your relationship to Canada's dynamic capital city will be deeper and more genuine.

Visa and Entry Requirements

Visa Exemptions: Citizens of a select group of nations are not required to get a visa in order to enter Canada for brief stays related to transit, business meetings, or tourism. The Visa Waiver Programme (VWP) includes these nations as visa-exempt members. If entering Canada via air, visitors from nations that do not need visas may do so with an Electronic Travel Authorization (eTA), or they may enter the country by land or water without one.

Visa-exempt foreign nationals entering Canada by plane must have an Electronic Travel Authorization (eTA), which is a prerequisite for admission. Before departing for Canada, visitors must submit an online application for an eTA. Typically, the procedure is simple and fast, but you must apply for the eTA well in advance of your intended departure date.

For brief travels to Canada, nationals of nations that are not exempt from visa requirements must apply for a Temporary Resident Visa (TRV), sometimes known as a visiting visa. The visitor visa permits entrance for travel, business, or visits to friends and relatives. The application procedure often includes providing the necessary paperwork, including a current passport, documentation of trip intentions, evidence of financial support, and other supplementary paperwork.

Study Permits and Work Permits: You must get the relevant study permit or work permit in addition to any required visas or eTAs if you wish to study or work in Canada.

Length of remain: The immigration officer at the point of entry typically decides how long a visitor may remain in Canada. Make sure your passport is still valid for the whole time you will be visiting Canada.

Medical Insurance: Most tourists to Canada are required to have current medical insurance for the length of their trip. Getting comprehensive travel insurance that offers medical protection, trip cancellation/interruption protection, and other travel-related benefits is advised.

Customs & Declarations: You must fill out a customs declaration form before entering Canada in order to list any products you are carrying.

Please keep in mind that immigration laws might change, so it is essential to confirm the most recent Canada visa and entrance requirements well in advance of your intended trip dates. The most dependable source of current information on visa and entrance requirements for Canada is the official website of Immigration, Refugees, and Citizenship Canada (IRCC).

EXPLORING OTTAWA'S HISTORY AND CULTURE

Indigenous Heritage

The Algonquin Anishinaabe Nation's historic unceded territory is where Ottawa, the nation's capital, is located. The history of the area is profoundly based in its indigenous heritage, which is still a vital component of Ottawa's cultural landscape. Here is a summary of Ottawa's rich Indigenous history and some suggestions for getting involved and appreciating it:

1. Acknowledging Indigenous History and Land: It's crucial to recognise and respect Ottawa's Indigenous heritage when you come. In order to acknowledge the Algonquin Anishinaabe Nation's traditional area and to show appreciation for their good management of the land, many public events, meetings, and official occasions start with a land recognition.

2. Ottawa is home to a number of museums and cultural institutions devoted to preserving and showcasing Indigenous history. Exhibits that showcase the history, art, and customs of Indigenous peoples in Canada may be seen in the

Canadian Museum of History, which is situated over the river in Gatineau, Quebec. For further information on Indigenous customs and services, check out the Wabano Centre for Aboriginal Health and the Odawa Native Friendship Centre.

3. Powwows and Indigenous Festivals: Ottawa organises a number of Indigenous events throughout the year, such as powwows and festivals that honour Indigenous dance, music, crafts, and cuisine. An excellent chance to interact with Indigenous people and learn about their rich traditions is to attend these events.

4. Native American art and craft galleries: Look into regional galleries and boutiques that include Native American paintings, sculptures, beading, and other traditional crafts. Supporting and promoting Indigenous artists and their communities may be accomplished by buying their work directly from them or via authorised dealers.

5. Traditional Indigenous Food: Look for eateries that serve food with an Indigenous influence, which often uses traditional ingredients and cooking methods. Indigenous cuisine offers not only a delicious culinary experience but also a window

into the culture's relationship with the environment.

6. Guided Tours and Workshops: Take part in a guided tour or workshop conducted by an Indigenous guide who will impart their expertise on the region's geography, history, and culture. These encounters provide a greater understanding of Indigenous viewpoints and practices.

7. Indigenous Language and Culture Programmes: To encourage the revival of Indigenous languages and practises, certain community centres and organisations provide Indigenous language lessons and cultural programmes. A significant approach to support the preservation of Indigenous heritage is through taking part in these programmes.

It's crucial to approach Ottawa's Indigenous legacy with respect, openness, and a readiness to learn. Understanding Indigenous cultures' history, customs, and current problems is essential to promoting respect and understanding amongst people. You may help larger attempts at reconciliation and recognition of Canada's Indigenous peoples and their substantial contributions to the identity and legacy of the country by upholding and honouring Indigenous customs.

Historic Sites and Landmarks

With a variety of historic structures and landmarks that provide a window into its past, Ottawa is a city steeped in history. Here are some of Ottawa's must-see historical buildings and landmarks, which range from impressive architectural marvels to major cultural and political milestones:

1. Parliament Hill: Located in the centre of Ottawa, Parliament Hill houses the federal government of Canada. It includes the magnificent East and West Blocks as well as the Peace Tower-emblazoned Centre Block. During the summer, visitors may participate in guided tours to learn about Canadian politics and history and see the Changing of the Guard event.

2. National War Memorial: The National War Memorial, which is located on Elgin Street, is a sombre and moving memorial to Canadian troops who sacrificed their lives in several wars. The monument is particularly important at yearly remembrance occasions like Remembrance Day.

3. Rideau Canal: The Rideau Canal, an engineering wonder and a significant waterway between Ottawa and Kingston, is included as a UNESCO World Heritage Site. The canal becomes the longest skating rink in the world in the winter, providing a unique and unforgettable experience.

4. ByWard Market: The ByWard Market, which goes back to the early 19th century, is one of Canada's oldest and liveliest public marketplaces. Today, it offers a diverse selection of stores, eateries, cafés, and a bustling ambiance, making it a well-liked attraction for both residents and tourists.

5. Canadian Museum of History: The Canadian Museum of History, which is located in Gatineau, Quebec, across the river, presents the history of the country's people, including Indigenous cultures, Canadian heritage, and pivotal moments that influenced the country.

6. Laurier House National Historic Site: Sir Wilfrid Laurier and William Lyon Mackenzie King previously called Laurier House their home. Learn about the lives and legacies of these significant men by exploring the beautifully conserved interiors.

7. Diefenbunker, Canada's Cold War Museum: The Diefenbunker is a former subterranean government building constructed during the Cold War and is located just outside of Ottawa. It has been turned into an interesting museum that provides details about Canada's involvement in the Cold War and its readiness for nuclear threats.

8. Notre-Dame Cathedral Basilica: One of Ottawa's most outstanding sights and a marvel of Gothic Revival design. The ornate interior of the cathedral has religious art and beautiful stained glass windows.

9. The Canadian Museum of Nature is situated in a spectacular structure that was constructed in 1912, however it is not truly historic. Fossils, minerals, and specimens of animals are just a few of the natural history exhibits on display at the museum.

10. Major's Hill Park: This historic park with a view of the Ottawa River and Parliament Hill is the ideal place for a leisurely walk, a picnic, or to take in outdoor performances and festivals.

These historical locations and monuments provide an enthralling tour through Ottawa's history and give visitors a greater appreciation of the country's political and cultural legacy. You will learn about the history and development of the country as you go to these amazing places and take in the architectural and cultural variety of the area.

Museums and Galleries

A culturally and historically significant city, Ottawa is home to a broad variety of museums and art galleries that appeal to a wide range of interests. There is a museum or gallery in Ottawa to pique your interest whether you are interested in art, history, science, or nature. Here are some of the best galleries and museums to visit:

1. National Gallery of Canada: The National Gallery of Canada is a renowned art gallery that is home to a remarkable collection of works by both Canadian and foreign artists. It includes a wide variety of artwork, including masterpieces created today as well as traditional Indigenous art. On the gallery's plaza outside, Louise Bourgeois' famous spider sculpture "Maman" stands prominent.

2. Canadian Museum of History: Situated in Gatineau, Quebec, right over the river, the Canadian Museum of History presents the history of the country via interesting exhibitions, artefacts,

and interactive displays. Discover Canadian history, Indigenous cultures, and pivotal moments that influenced the nation.

3. Canadian Museum of Nature: At the Canadian Museum of Nature, explore the marvels of the natural world. The museum is home to a sizable collection of dinosaur fossils in addition to other items such as animals, birds, minerals, and rocks.

4. Canadian War Museum: The Canadian War Museum is a great place to learn about the military history of Canada and the contributions made by its armed forces. This museum is home to a sizable collection of artefacts, souvenirs, and exhibitions commemorating the exploits and sacrifices of Canadian troops.

5. Canada Aviation and Space Museum: Visitors to the Canada Aviation and Space Museum will be enthralled. The remarkable collection of historic aeroplanes, helicopters, and interactive displays at this museum highlights the development of aviation in Canada.

6. Ottawa Art Gallery: The OAG is committed to promoting modern Canadian art, especially those by artists from the Ottawa-Gatineau area. The OAG

often presents open programmes and rotating exhibits to honour the regional cultural scene.

7. Bytown Museum: The Bytown Museum, situated close to the Rideau Canal, offers information about Ottawa's past. The museum explores the early years of Ottawa's growth and the building of the Rideau Canal, providing insights into the history of the city.

8. Canadian Science and Technology Museum: Visit the Canadian Science and Technology Museum to learn more about the world of science and technology. This interactive museum offers interesting displays on a range of scientific fields and technology advancements.

9. Bank of Canada Museum: Visit the Bank of Canada Museum to delve into the worlds of money and economics. This museum presents a distinctive viewpoint on the economy of Canada and the function of the Bank of Canada.

10. Portrait Gallery of Canada: Through portraits and multimedia exhibitions, the Portrait Gallery of Canada honours the contributions and accomplishments of notable Canadians. It provides an enthralling visual account of the country's varied cultural environment.

These museums and galleries are just a handful of Ottawa's many cultural attractions. Inspiring and thought-provoking experiences are offered by Ottawa's museums and galleries for visitors of all ages and interests, regardless of their passions for art, history, science, or any other subject.

DISCOVERING OTTAWA'S NEIGHBOURHOOD

Downtown Ottawa

From historical sites to busy avenues lined with stores and restaurants, downtown Ottawa is a lively and dynamic location that provides a varied variety of activities. Sparks Street and Elgin Street are two significant landmarks in downtown Ottawa.

1. Sparks Street: One of Ottawa's most well-known pedestrian malls and one of the city's oldest streets, Sparks Street is noteworthy historically. It is located close to Parliament Hill and extends between Elgin Street and Lyon Street, parallel to Wellington Street. What to anticipate to discover on Sparks Street is as follows:

- Dining and Shopping: Sparks Street is a well-known spot for dining and shopping since it is home to a wide selection of stores, boutiques, and cafés. There are many possibilities to explore, whether you're seeking stylish apparel, unusual presents, or a delicious dinner.

- Outdoor Events: Sparks Street holds a wide variety of outdoor events, festivals, and street performances throughout the year. On this lively boulevard, there's always something going on, from music festivals to cultural festivities.

- Landmarks: The Bank of Canada's main office, a superb example of Beaux-Arts architecture, is one of the exquisite heritage buildings that decorate Sparks Street, which is considered a landmark because of its historical importance.

2. Elgin Street: From Wellington Street to the Queen Elizabeth Driveway, Elgin Street runs north-south through the heart of downtown Ottawa. What you can discover on Elgin Street is as follows:

Elgin Street is recognised for its dynamic and diversified food scene, which includes a wide variety of eateries, cafés, and pubs. Elgin Street offers a variety of dining options, whether you're craving a cosy pub, delicious foreign food, or something more hearty from Canada.

- Cultural Attractions: The National Arts Centre (NAC), Canada's top performing arts facility, is one of several cultural institutions that call Elgin Street home. Numerous concerts, musicals, dance performances, and other creative events are held at the NAC.

- Festivals & Special Events: Elgin Street is a lively place for entertainment and festivities during festivals and other special events.

- Green Spaces: Confederation Park, a beautiful park that holds events and provides a peaceful haven in the middle of the city, is not far from the southern end of Elgin Street.

Both Sparks Street and Elgin Street provide distinctive experiences and highlight the variety of options available in downtown Ottawa. These two streets give a look of the dynamic lifestyle and attractions that the downtown region has to offer, from historical sites and cultural institutions to shopping, restaurants, and exciting events.

The Glebe

Welcome to The Glebe, a lovely area located just south of Ottawa, the nation's capital. The Glebe is a compelling location that provides a beautiful mix of traditional charm and contemporary vibrancy. It is steeped in history and decorated with a strong sense of community.

1. Historical Foundations and Elegant Architecture: You can't help but be fascinated by The Glebe's ancient origins as you meander through its tree-lined lanes. Elegant homes from the Victorian and Edwardian eras that still survive in the area are a tribute to its illustrious past and preserve the history of the city in their elaborate façade. You are immediately transported to a moment of timeless beauty by the overt historical sense.

2. Lansdowne Park: The Centre of the Neighbourhood: Lansdowne Park, a vibrant and alluring attraction that appeals to both residents and tourists, is located in the centre of The Glebe. A wonderful fusion of residential, business, and recreational areas can be found in the freshly revitalised park, which has transformed into a lively meeting spot. It's exciting and friendly when you watch a spectacular CFL football game at TD Place Stadium or browse the many unique boutiques and businesses nearby.

3. Delicious Shopping and Dining: The Glebe's main street, Bank Street, is a sanctuary for foodies and shoppers alike. The Boulevard is lined with unusual boutiques, specialised shops and small companies, each of which offers a treasure trove of

chic treasures, handcrafted items and original presents. The variety of dining options, from hip restaurants to cosy cafés serving delicious international cuisine, will thrill foodies.

4. Farmers' Market at Lansdowne, A Feast for the Senses: The Lansdowne Farmers' Market comes alive on weekends, luring customers in with an array of locally produced goods, gourmet treats, and fresh fruit. The fragrances of handmade items permeate the air, luring tourists to taste and enjoy the greatest regional flavours. The market is a celebration of the diverse food culture of the area as well as a paradise for foodies.

5. Peaceful Escapes Among Urban Activity: The Glebe provides peaceful retreats in its natural areas despite the rush of city life. With its lovely pond and winding trails, Patterson Creek Park offers a tranquil haven for rest and reflection. Along the historic Rideau Canal, Brown's Inlet Park provides breathtaking vistas and a tranquil atmosphere, making it the ideal setting for leisurely strolls or quiet periods of introspection.

6. Community spirit and cohesion: A tight-knit community that relies on its feeling of camaraderie, The Glebe is more than simply a neighbourhood.

The Glebe Community Centre, which offers a wide range of leisure, educational, and cultural programmes that unite locals and guests, acts as the neighbourhood's beating heart. The centre promotes a friendly and inviting atmosphere for everyone via exercise programmes, art workshops, and community activities.

7. Celebrations & Festivals: The Glebe vibrates with enthusiasm all year long as it serves as the venue for several events and festivities. The neighbourhood is brightened and made happier through art displays, musical performances, and get-togethers for families. These activities create treasured memories for both residents and tourists and are a reflection of The Glebe's thriving sense of community.

8. A Beautiful Farewell: You leave The Glebe with a feeling of magic and a connection to its alluring tapestry of history, culture, and community. Your heart is forever changed by the area's enduring charm, magnificent architecture, and vibrant environment. The Glebe is a hidden gem in the centre of Ottawa that welcomes everyone who comes to discover its distinctive appeal and join its friendly community.

Little Italy in the Heart of Ottawa

Welcome to Little Italy, a bustling and charming area tucked away in the centre of Ottawa, the nation's capital. As soon as you enter this energetic neighbourhood, you'll be whisked away to an Italian-inspired setting where the enticing fragrances of cappuccino and freshly baked pastries fill the air and the friendliness of the locals welcome you like an old acquaintance.

1. Italian Cultural Delights and Heritage: Every element of the neighbourhood in Little Italy celebrates Italian ancestry and culture. The buildings' vibrant façade, which are decorated with Italian flags and lovely paintings, provide a gorgeous scene that is evocative of the sleepy towns in Italy. The community's rich Italian heritage is reflected in the rituals, language, and traditions that are shared with guests and tenderly maintained.

2. Genuine culinary encounters: The gastronomic choices of Little Italy, where the tastes of Italy come to life, are one of its attractions. The streets are lined with quaint cafés, family-owned pizzerias, and traditional trattorias, all tempting you with cuisine

that will take your taste buds to Florence or Rome. The food experience in Little Italy is a feast for the senses, with everything from traditional pasta meals to delicious gelato.

3. Preston Street: Little Italy's main road, Preston Street, serves as the vibrant centre of this little community. The street beckons you to discover its hidden gems since it is lined with charming businesses, specialised stores and beautiful boutiques. Preston Street guarantees a pleasurable shopping experience, whether you're looking for distinctive Italian mementos or are just indulging in retail therapy.

4. Lively Festivals and Events: Little Italy comes alive with a calendar full of exciting occasions and celebrations of the spirit and culture of Italy. An annual highlight is the Italian Week Festival, which includes delicious Italian food as well as music, dancing, and other visual and performing arts. Every visit to Little Italy is a special and joyful affair because of the neighbourhood's contagious atmosphere of celebration.

5. Community and hospitable behaviour: You'll experience a strong feeling of community and kind welcome as you wander through Little Italy's

picturesque streets. The locals are proud of their Italian background and want to tell guests about it. You'll feel welcomed and embraced by the neighbourhood's warm vibe, whether you strike up a discussion with a local at a café or participate in a fun street event.

6. Ottawa's glimpses of Italy: Little Italy is more than simply a neighbourhood; it's a point of contact between many cultures that introduces a touch of Italy to Ottawa. A wealth of Italian customs, music, and art may be found as you stroll through its picturesque streets, adding romance and authenticity to the city's international atmosphere.

7. An Experience To Remember: A trip to Little Italy is a once-in-a-lifetime event that permanently changes you. The area gives a taste of Italy's charm right in the centre of Ottawa, whether you want to indulge in the delectable tastes of Italian food or immerse yourself in the rich cultural legacy. So come and enjoy Little Italy's warmth and charm, where the romance of the country's cultural past permeates every second.

Hintonburg

Welcome to Hintonburg, a bustling and artistic district tucked away in the centre of Ottawa, the nation's capital. Hintonburg invites tourists to explore its varied selection of galleries, shops, and bustling streets. The neighbourhood is known for its creative flare, unique appeal, and sense of community.

1. Cultural diversity and the artistic community: Hintonburg is a hive of innovation, with a lively neighbourhood of musicians, artists, and craftspeople. The vibrant murals that decorate the neighbourhood's buildings and convert the streets into an outdoor art exhibit give away the area's creative spirit. Hintonburg's rich cultural legacy is commemorated via a variety of activities and festivals that highlight the skills of regional performers and artists.

2. Shops and galleries: You may find a treasure trove of one-of-a-kind shops and art galleries as you stroll through Hintonburg. The area is a sanctuary for art lovers, featuring a variety of modern and traditional artworks, handcrafted goods, and unique items. Hintonburg offers something for every art enthusiast, whether you're seeking for a

one-of-a-kind gift or want to be inspired by the local talent.

3. Wellington Street West: Hintonburg's main thoroughfare, Wellington Street West, is teeming with vitality and inventiveness. The street is a centre of activity, lined with local stores, cafés, and eateries that highlight the unique character of the neighbourhood. Discover the various choices of Wellington Street West, which range from inviting bookshops to chic designer businesses.

4. Gastronomic adventures and culinary delights: Hintonburg has a rich culinary culture that appeals to all tastes and preferences, making it a food lover's delight. The area offers a unique culinary experience with everything from cutting-edge farm-to-table restaurants to quaint diners offering foreign cuisine. Hintonburg is a unique culinary destination because of its use of fresh, locally sourced ingredients, inventive flavours, and dedication to quality.

5. Park areas and public gatherings: A close-knit community that takes pride in its open spaces and recreational options, Hintonburg is more than simply a neighbourhood. Locals and tourists alike congregate at parks including Parkdale Park and

Somerset Square, which also host festivals, fairs, and community activities. The welcoming atmosphere promotes interactions and a strong feeling of community.

6. Supporting Local Businesses and Sustainable Living: Hintonburg upholds the ideals of sustainable living and local business support. Numerous stores and companies place a high value on using eco-friendly procedures and locally produced goods, adding to the neighbourhood's distinctive character and encouraging a feeling of social responsibility.

7. A Special and Motivating Experience: In Hintonburg, where art, culture, and community come together to create a vibrant and friendly environment, visitors can expect a one-of-a-kind and inspirational experience. Hintonburg welcomes you to immerse yourself in its artistic sanctuary and enjoy the creative energy that pours through its streets, whether you're visiting the art galleries, trying out various cuisines, or just taking in the colourful street life.

Westboro

Welcome to Westboro, a vibrant and fashionable urban community situated on the Ottawa River's western bank. This bustling neighbourhood offers a lively environment and a wealth of activities for locals and guests alike. It is the ideal combination of contemporary style and neighbourhood charm.

1. Fashionable Shops and Shopping Extravaganzas: With its wide selection of chic boutiques and cutting-edge stores, Westboro is a fashionista's dream come true. Fashionable options in the area include trendy designer apparel, distinctive accessories, and regionally produced handicrafts to suit a variety of interests. The shops in Westboro provide a fun shopping experience, whether you're looking for the newest fashion trends or a one-of-a-kind item.

2. Culinary hotspots and trendy cafes: Westboro is a delight for foodies with its streets dotted with quaint cafés and fine dining establishments. The neighbourhood's food culture is a fantastic excursion, with everything from artisanal coffee shops to foreign restaurants offering exquisite cuisine. Each dining experience is a genuine gourmet joy since local chefs take satisfaction in

utilising seasonal, fresh foods that are acquired nearby.

3. The central area of Westboro is Wellington Street West: Westboro's busy centre, Wellington Street West, is where the area's urban vitality comes to life. The Boulevard is dotted with lively stores, boutiques, and restaurants, creating a vibrant and varied atmosphere. Wellington Street West is the ideal spot to take a leisurely stroll or meet up with friends because of the sidewalk patios and outdoor sitting places that create a vibrant street scene.

4. Beautiful parks and retreats along the rivers: Due to Westboro's closeness to the Ottawa River, lovely parks and riverfront getaways are possible. Beautiful river views can be found at Westboro Beach and Riverfront Park, which also offers a tranquil respite from the hustle and bustle of the city. Both locals and tourists love having picnics, going kayaking, and taking leisurely strolls along the river's side.

5. Culture and the Arts Scene: Westboro encourages creativity in the community by embracing art and culture. Exhibitions of artwork, live performances, and cultural activities that highlight local talent and promote the arts are held in the neighbourhood.

The streets of the neighbourhood are given a creative touch by public art installations and neighbourhood murals.

6. Active Way of Life and Recreation: Westboro's abundance of fitness centres, gyms, and outdoor leisure areas encourage an active way of life. Residents of the area value health and wellbeing and like remaining active by participating in a variety of activities, such as riding along beautiful routes or doing yoga in a local park.

7. Events and Community Engagement: The vibrant activities and gatherings in Westboro are evidence of the area's strong feeling of community. Seasonal festivals, farmers' markets, and neighbourhood fairs are held throughout the area, bringing neighbours together and fostering an atmosphere that is inviting and inclusive to everyone.

8. Experience A Vibrant Urban Village: Westboro provides a lively and stylish urban village experience where residents and guests may take advantage of the best of both worlds: sophisticated and contemporary living amongst a warm and inviting neighbourhood. Westboro welcomes you to embrace its urban charm and make enduring memories in this stylish and vibrant

neighbourhood, whether you're perusing the chic stores, indulging in the culinary treats, or just admiring the picturesque riverbank.

Chinatown

Welcome to Chinatown, a thriving and culturally diverse area in the centre of Ottawa, the nation's capital. You will be swept away into the vibrant and enthralling world of Chinese culture as soon as you enter this busy neighbourhood, where the sights, sounds, and tastes combine to provide a genuine experience.

1. Gateway to Chinese culture: As the gateway to Chinese culture, Chinatown's elaborate archways decorated with traditional Chinese motifs welcome visitors to this alluring neighbourhood. You'll feel a strong feeling of tradition and heritage and get completely engrossed in the wealth of Chinese rituals and traditions.

2. Asian food and culinary treats: The delicious food scene in Chinatown is one of its attractions. Asian foods are abundant in the area, from savoury dim sum to rich Szechuan meals, making it a foodie's heaven. Each restaurant offers a tempting cuisine

that entices you to go through the many flavours of the Far East.

3. Genuine Asian markets and stores: Markets and businesses that highlight the finest of Asian items and products line the busy streets of Chinatown. Traditional herbal shops, bustling fruit markets and specialty businesses selling rare spices and teas may all be found there. These stores are a gold mine for anybody looking for unusual products and items from Asian cultures.

4. Cultural Festivals and Events: Cultural activities and festivals bring Chinatown to life and highlight the vivacious energy of the neighbourhood. A lot of energy is put into the celebration of holidays like Chinese New Year and the Mid-Autumn Festival, which include vibrant parades, dragon dances, and firecrackers that enliven the atmosphere.

5. Cultural Goodwill and Hospitality: Chinatown has a strong feeling of belonging among its citizens, which is reflected in the neighbourhood's inviting atmosphere. Whether you are a visiting or a resident, you will be welcomed with open arms and a warm smile. Residents of the area take delight in introducing outsiders to their culture and customs, making every interaction joyful.

6. Historical Sites and Gardens: Many historical sites, like temples and gardens, can be found in Chinatown, which adds to the appeal of the area. The Chinatown Gateway, a famous archway, is a towering representation of harmony and ethnic pride. A tranquil haven in the middle of the bustling city is the Chinese Garden.

7. Chinatown's Development: Chinatown has developed through time into a vibrant and varied neighbourhood that welcomes not just members of the Chinese community but also people from other ethnic backgrounds. Chinatown is now a microcosm of Ottawa's ethnic character because of the blending of cultures that this development has produced.

8. An Ottawa Cultural Expedition: A trip to Chinatown is more than simply a leisurely walk around a neighbourhood; it's also an immersion in the local culture. Chinatown welcomes you to experience the rich tapestry of Chinese history and make unforgettable memories while exploring the bustling streets, indulging in genuine food, or taking part in cultural activities.

ENJOYING OTTAWA'S NATURAL BEAUTY

Gatineau Park

Gatineau Park, a 360 square km expanse of pristine and diversified natural habitat, is just a short drive from the city of Ottawa. This gorgeous park provides a variety of activities and attractions for families, nature lovers, and adventurers. Gatineau Park should be on your must-visit list for the following reasons:

1. Trails for Every Adventurer: Discover the extensive system of hiking routes that are appropriate for all ability levels. Every path offers panoramic views of shimmering lakes, lush woods, and rolling hills, ranging from simple strolls to strenuous treks.

2. Scenic Lookouts: Gatineau Park is home to a variety of vantage points that provide mesmerising views of the surroundings. Take breathtaking panorama pictures that reach far into the distance.

3. Pink Lake's Distinctive Beauty Experience Pink Lake's captivating turquoise waters, known for their particular colour brought on by mineral deposits.

Discover the lake's geological history and ecological significance.

4. Magic of Winter Wonderland: Accept the winter paradise that, in the cooler months, envelops Gatineau Park. Enjoy tranquil snowshoe excursions through snow-covered woodlands or cross-country skiing on groomed tracks.

5. The Lusk Cave adventure: Lusk Cave provides a subterranean adventure for the intrepid and interested. Explore the confined spaces and fascinating rock formations in this geological wonder.

6. Wildlife Encounters: Gatineau Park is home to a wide variety of animals. As you explore their natural habitats, keep a close watch out for white-tailed deer, beavers, foxes, and a wide range of bird species.

7. The estate of Mackenzie King: At the Mackenzie King Estate, the former summer home of Prime Minister William Lyon Mackenzie King, you can immerse yourself in Canadian history. Wander through magical gardens and get a glimpse of the past.

The closeness of Gatineau Park to Ottawa makes it a perfect getaway from the city, offering a refuge of natural delights just outside the municipal borders. Gatineau Park provides an exceptional experience that will fascinate you, whether you're looking for outdoor activities, quiet tranquilly, or a look into Canada's history. Plan your trip right now to take in the splendour of this natural haven close to Ottawa.

Major's Hill Park

Major's Hill Park, located in the centre of downtown Ottawa, provides a beautiful fusion of deep history and stunning landscape. This famous park has grown to be a beloved destination for both residents and visitors. It is set on a hill overlooking the lovely Ottawa River and Parliament Hill. Following are some convincing reasons to include Major's Hill Park on your itinerary:

1. Historical Importance: Learn about the park's past as one of Ottawa's first public areas. It originally housed military defences and has been the scene of significant events in Canada's history.

2. Amazing Views: Enjoy unmatched panoramic views of the city's cityscape, the Ottawa River, and the famous Parliament Buildings. Take

picture-perfect pictures while admiring the views from different vantage points.

3. Year-round celebrations: Major's Hill Park is a hive of activity all year round. There's always something spectacular going on in this dynamic public area, from colourful festivals and cultural events to outdoor concerts and art displays.

4. Serenity in the Natural World: Enjoy a leisurely stroll over well maintained lawns, colourful flower beds, and shady walkways. The calm atmosphere of the park provides a much-needed break from the busy city streets.

5. Ideal Picnic Location: Take a picnic and take in the stunning scenery all around you. Major's Hill Park offers the ideal backdrop for a leisurely outdoor lunch, whether it's a date or a family adventure.

6. Closeness to ByWard Market: The park is close to the bustling ByWard Market, allowing you to easily transition from eating and shopping to tranquil leisure in the middle of nature.

7. Skating in the winter: Major's Hill Park changes into a winter wonderland when Ottawa is covered

with snow in the winter. Put on your skates, glide around the picturesque outdoor ice rink, and spin around while you take it all in.

Major's Hill Park offers a chance to see Ottawa's natural beauty up close and take a trip back in time. Major's Hill Park will make a lasting effect on your time in Ottawa, whether you're researching the historical features, taking in the stunning surroundings, or just looking for a quiet retreat.

Rideau Falls

Within a short drive of Ottawa's downtown, the spectacular Rideau Falls attracts tourists with its breathtaking grandeur and thundering waterfalls. This famous site, where the Rideau River and the Ottawa River converge, provides a tranquil respite from the hustle and bustle of the city while also offering a window into Canada's extensive history. The following reasons make a trip to Rideau Falls a necessity on your agenda for Ottawa:

1. Awe-inspiring Waterfalls: Be in awe of the stunning scene of the cascading streams crashing into the Ottawa River. The beautiful and powerful show of nature's force is created by the flowing waterfall.

2. Scenic Lookout Points: You may observe the falls from a variety of perspectives thanks to many strategically placed observation platforms. Take the ideal shot or just relax and take in the tranquillity of the running river and green surroundings.

3. Historical value: As the beginning of the Rideau Canal, a UNESCO World Heritage Site and an engineering wonder that was crucial to the early development of Canada, Rideau Falls has historical value.

4. Walking Routes: Take a leisurely stroll around the falls on one of the several walking pathways. Enjoy a tranquil getaway while taking in the area's rich animals and natural beauty.

5. Closeness to government structures: The falls' advantageous position makes it possible to explore surrounding government facilities and sites, including the National Research Council and the Prime Minister's house at 24 Sussex Drive.

6. Year-Round Appeal: Rideau Falls draws tourists all year long. The region transforms into a tranquil paradise for picnics and leisure during the summer

months, while in the winter, the frozen falls provide a stunning background for brisk hikes.

Boat excursions and cruises: To come up close to the falls and get a different viewpoint of this natural beauty, think about going on a boat trip or cruise down the Ottawa River.

Rideau Falls offers a captivating synthesis of scenic beauty and historical importance. The falls provide a really memorable experience that captures the very best of Ottawa's charm and beauty, whether you're a nature lover, history buff, or just looking for a quiet getaway. When you visit the Canadian capital, don't pass up the opportunity to see this natural beauty.

Dow's Lake

Dow's Lake, a calm refuge that welcomes tourists with its serene beauty and a variety of recreational opportunities, lies tucked away in the centre of Ottawa. This lovely urban lake provides the ideal getaway for nature lovers, outdoor explorers, and those seeking quiet leisure. It is located close to well-known attractions and neighbourhoods.

1. Scenic Beauty: Enjoy Dow's Lake's stunning surroundings of lush vegetation, vibrant flower beds, and tranquil waters. The exquisite landscape around the lake makes for a beautiful background for leisurely strolls and quiet reflection.

2. A Wide Range of Activities: Whether you like canoeing, kayaking, or paddle boarding, Dow's Lake has a range of water sports for people of all ages and experience levels. Take your time paddling around the serene waters of the lake on a rented boat.

3. Wintertime Skating: Dow's Lake morphs into a beautiful ice-skating haven in the winter. Skate down the frozen lake while gliding through the surrounding winter splendour.

4. Tulip Festival: The famed Canadian Tulip Festival in Ottawa is centred around Dow's Lake, where thousands of vivid tulips bloom, producing a dazzling display that honours Canada's affinity with the Netherlands.

5. Restaurants and coffee shops: Take pleasure in delicious eating occasions at the lakeside eateries. Enjoy wonderful meals while gazing out over the

sea, which will enhance the atmosphere of your trip.

6. Paths for biking and walking: Take leisurely strolls or bike rides around Dow's Lake on the nearby pathways. The beautiful pathways provide chances to experience the lake's unspoiled splendour while being active.

7. Nearness to Attractions: Dow's Lake is an excellent place to stop on your sightseeing excursions since it is conveniently placed close to several of Ottawa's major attractions, including the Canadian Museum of Nature, Lansdowne Park, and the vibrant Glebe neighbourhood.

Dow's Lake is a must-see location in Ottawa because it successfully combines urban convenience with natural tranquillity. A trip to Dow's Lake will leave you feeling rejuvenated and enchanted by the allure of this urban paradise, whether you're taking advantage of the water sports, savouring the seasonal tulip blossoms, or just relaxing in nature's embrace.

Experimental Farm

For nature lovers and inquisitive minds alike, the Central Experimental Farm, a botanical haven situated in the centre of Ottawa, provides a unique and rewarding experience. This renowned agricultural research facility, run by Agriculture and Agri-Food Canada, highlights the marvels of horticulture, academic inquiry, and environmentally friendly farming methods. Here are some reasons why you absolutely must include a trip to Canada's Experimental Farm on your schedule for Ottawa:

1. Lush Gardens: Discover many beautifully designed gardens that each highlight various plant species and horticulture practices. The Experimental Farm is a horticultural marvel with everything from vibrant flower displays to peaceful rock gardens.

2. Garden ornaments: Explore the Ornamental Gardens, a mesmerising display of painstakingly crafted flowerbeds, lovely walkways, and beautiful plants that vary with the seasons.

3. The arboretum is a kind of park. Explore the Arboretum to learn about various species from

across the world. It supports a diverse range of trees and plants.

4. Domesticated animals: At the Agriculture Museum, a facility on the Experimental Farm, you may pet friendly farm animals. Children and adults alike will enjoy the chance to engage with animals and discover what it's like to live on a farm.

5. Educational Displays: Participate in educational exhibitions that feature the most recent agricultural research and sustainable farming techniques. Learn about the role that science and technology play in environmental protection and food production.

6. Picnic Locations: Bring a picnic, and take your time eating lunch while taking in the park-like scenery. There are many beautiful places to unwind and enjoy your dinner.

7. Photography Possibilities: The Experimental Farm offers various opportunities for photographers to take beautiful shots of the flowers, animals, and attractive settings, so they will feel right at home there.

The Central Experimental Farm provides an enthralling combination of learning, entertainment, and the beauty of nature. This floral gem offers a special experience that honours Canada's dedication to horticultural excellence and environmental care, whether you're a gardening enthusiast, a family looking for a fun excursion, or someone interested in learning about sustainable agriculture.

Greenbelt and Trails

A haven for outdoor enthusiasts, the Ottawa Greenbelt and its vast network of trails provide a pleasant escape from the bustle of the city and a wealth of opportunities for outdoor recreation. The city's protective green belt offers a sanctuary for animals, outdoor lovers, and those looking for peace and quiet. The Ottawa Greenbelt and its trails should be on your must-visit list for the following reasons:

1. Significant Green Spaces: Explore the wide area of vegetation that stretches across the city's fringes, which includes woods, ponds, and meadows. The Greenbelt offers a chance to re-establish contact with nature and serves as a refuge for a variety of animals.

2. A significant trail network: Explore a wide variety of pathways suited for cycling, jogging, hiking, and

nature hikes. Choose from a variety of routes that give different vantage points of Ottawa's natural beauty, ranging from short and relaxing to longer and more difficult.

3. Greenbelt Discovery Walks: Discover the Greenbelt with its self-guided walking excursions, the Greenbelt Discovery Walks, which take you to a variety of natural and historical sites. Learn about the region's significant environmental history and rich legacy.

4. Winter Wonderland: Enjoy the winter splendour that the Greenbelt turns into when the weather gets colder. Opportunities for cross-country skiing, snowshoeing, and winter hiking abound, enabling you to experience the tranquillity of nature in a brand-new way.

5. Areas for Picnics and Recreation: Family trips, picnics, and barbecues may be enjoyed in a variety of approved picnic spots and recreational locations. Spend quality time with loved ones while taking in the beautiful scenery.

6. NCC Greenbelt Pathway: The NCC Greenbelt Pathway, a well-maintained network of interconnecting paths that provides simple

navigation and accessibility for all users, crisscrosses the Greenbelt.

7. Experiencing Wildlife: As you explore the Greenbelt's natural ecosystems, keep a look out for a variety of animals, including deer, foxes, birds, and numerous small mammals.

Numerous possibilities exist to explore, have fun, and appreciate nature's beauty in the Ottawa Greenbelt and its enormous trail system. The Greenbelt and its paths will leave you with treasured memories of Ottawa's abundant natural playground, whether you're looking for adventure, quiet reflection, or an opportunity to witness animals in their natural home.

FAMILY-FRIENDLY ACTIVITIES IN OTTAWA

Canadian Museum of Science and Technology

A fascinating venue that honours Canada's rich scientific background and technical advances is the Canadian Museum of Science and Technology in Ottawa. This interactive museum showcases the marvels of science, engineering, and invention and provides a wonderful experience for visitors of all ages. The Canadian Museum of Science and Technology must be seen when you are in Ottawa for the following reasons:

1. Hands-On exhibitions: Participate in interactive exhibitions that promote learning and discovery. Visitors are encouraged to let their curiosity run wild and engage in the marvels of science via interactive exhibits and scientific presentations.

2. Innovation Alley: Discover Canadian ideas that have influenced the contemporary world at Innovation Alley, where you can immerse yourself in the dynamic world of innovation.

3. Steam engine demonstrations: During live steam engine demonstrations, you may marvel at the impressive strength of a moving steam locomotive as it rumbles around the rails.

4. Vintage vehicles and modes of transportation: A collection of historic automobiles, railways and aircraft that have been important to Canada's growth will help you learn about the country's transportation history.

5. Children's Museum: The museum has a separate Children's Museum with engaging displays intended to pique children's interest and encourage a love of science and technology.

6. Special Showcases: The museum often presents special exhibits that explore a range of topics in science, technology, and innovation. To find out what fascinating exhibits are scheduled for your visit, check the schedule.

7. Outdoor objects: Explore the museum's outdoor display area, which includes bigger artefacts from Canada's industrial history, including antique trains and industrial gear.

The Canadian Museum of Science and Technology is a venue where learning and enjoyment collide, giving visitors a fascinating way to learn about Canada's scientific and technology advancements. The museum offers an educational and inspirational experience that celebrates the glories of human creativity and adventure, whether you're a scientific enthusiast, a history buff, or someone seeking for a family-friendly trip.

Canada Aviation and Space Museum

An exciting voyage into the fascinating worlds of aviation and space exploration is provided by the Canada Aviation and Space Museum in Ottawa. With its outstanding collection of vintage aircraft, interactive exhibitions, and immersive experiences, this top museum celebrates Canada's rich aerospace legacy. Aviation lovers, space enthusiasts, and history buffs alike must visit this fascinating museum. What to expect at the Canada Aviation and Space Museum is as follows:

1. Historical Aircraft Collection: Admire a wide variety of painstakingly restored vintage aeroplanes from various eras of aviation. The museum's collection charts the development of aviation

technology, from recognisable biplanes to famed jet fighters.

2. Innovation in Aviation: Experience the creativity and invention of Canadian pioneers in aviation. Find out about their industry-changing accomplishments and efforts.

3. Avro Arrow, The Iconic Aircraft: The Avro Arrow, a storied Canadian aeroplane that represents innovation and the quest of perfection in aviation design, should inspire awe.

4. Interactive displays: Participate in interactive displays that provide practical learning opportunities. Explore cockpit models, put your flying talents to the test, and learn the physics behind space and air travel.

5. Space Exploration: Take a historical journey through space exploration to learn about Canada's contributions to satellite technology and space missions.

6. Outdoor Aircraft Park: Head outdoors to check out the outdoor aircraft park, where you can get up close to even more aircraft, such as helicopters,

military planes, and a full-scale replica of the renowned Avro Arrow.

7. Astronomy and Beyond: Explore the marvels of the cosmos and the universe with enthralling exhibits on astronomy, celestial objects, and the most recent space discoveries.

The Canada Aviation and Space Museum is a fascinating attraction that honours Canada's accomplishments in the aerospace industry and the spirit of exploration in general. This museum promises an awe-inspiring journey that highlights the triumphs and challenges of human exploration and the extraordinary machines that have taken us to the skies and beyond, whether you're an aviation enthusiast, a space aficionado, or simply curious about the wonders of flight and space travel.

Ottawa Children's Festival

The Ottawa Children's Festival is a wonderful and frivolous occasion that delights both young and young-at-heart people with enchantment and wonder. This charming event, which takes place every year in the centre of Canada's capital, is a must-see attraction for families visiting Ottawa. The festival, which attracts families from near and far, provides a variety of engrossing performances, interactive workshops, and outdoor activities that have been especially chosen to inspire children of all ages' imaginations and inventiveness.

1. A Universe of Theatrical Marvels: As renowned artists from all over the globe hit the stage, get ready to be transported to a world filled with theatrical delights. Each event is designed to mesmerise and fascinate young audiences, leaving them wide-eyed with amazement. These shows may include intriguing puppetry, enthralling storytelling, or high-energy musical performances.

2. Interactive Workshops that Inspire: Encourage your child's developing creativity via a range of engaging programmes. These interactive classes expose kids to the worlds of arts and crafts, dance, music, and storytelling under the direction of accomplished artists. Observe as their creativity soars as they bring their own original creations to life.

3. Outdoor Play and Adventures: The event provides a variety of outdoor activities and playground possibilities for families to enjoy, all set against the background of beautiful landscapes.

Enjoy outdoor activities like playing games and taking leisurely walks among the stunning scenery while you picnic beneath the stars.

4. An exploration of cultural diversity: The Ottawa Children's Festival showcases exciting performances and activities from all around the world to promote cultural diversity. Children have the opportunity to encounter the diversity of international arts, traditions, and customs, building an awareness for the rich fabric of cultural diversity around the globe.

5. Making Indelible Memories: The festival's welcoming environment for families fosters friendship and shared experiences. Indulging in a world of imagination and wonder, both parents and kids make priceless experiences that they will enjoy for years to come.

6. Beautiful interactive installations: As kids discover interactive art exhibits that promote inquiry and involvement, their curiosity is sparked. These fascinating displays provide a feast for the senses and fill young brains with creativity.

7. A Learning Journey: The Ottawa Children's Festival provides important educational opportunities in addition to entertainment. Children are exposed to a variety of artistic mediums, cultural customs, and the creative process, increasing their educational experience.

The Ottawa Children's Festival is a must-visit location for families looking for a wonderfully enchanted experience in Ottawa. It encourages creativity and enthuses young brains as it celebrates the pleasures of childhood. The festival's enchanted atmosphere, mesmerising performances, and engaging events make sure that the young explorers who attend leave with hearts full of wonder and treasured memories. Don't pass up the chance to experience this whimsical journey while you are in Ottawa. This festival honours the incredible charm of children and the limitless potential of the arts.

Parks and Playgrounds

There are several parks and playgrounds in Ottawa, making it the ideal place for outdoor activities, relaxation, and family fun. These parks have something to offer everyone, whether you're a nature lover, a fitness fanatic, or a family looking to spend some quality time outside. Here are some reasons you should put visiting Ottawa's parks and playgrounds on your to-do list:

1. Natural Beauty and Calmness: Discover the peace of Ottawa's parks, where lush vegetation, quiet lakes, and meandering pathways entice you to lose yourself in the embrace of nature. These green areas provide a haven from the bustle of the city and invite you to relax and refuel.

2. Family-friendly entertainment: The parks and playgrounds in Ottawa are a source of happiness and fun for families with small children. Little ones may let loose their energy and imagination in safe and creative play areas that include everything from climbing structures and swings to slides and splash pads.

3. Picnics and recreation: Take a picnic basket with you and visit the parks for some outdoor eating while taking in the stunning scenery. Numerous parks provide open areas with picnic tables where you may spend quality time with family and friends.

4. Fitness and recreation: Ottawa's parks offer a lot to those who like staying in shape. Join a yoga class outside, go for a run along the beautiful paths, play

some football or volleyball with some friends on the wide fields.

5. Geographic Lookouts: You may find picturesque lookouts in certain parks, which reward you with panoramic views of the Ottawa River, the city skyline, or stunning sunsets. Remember to bring your camera so you can record these picture-perfect moments.

6. Seasonal Favourites: Some parks are transformed into winter wonderlands in the winter, complete with cross-country skiing tracks and ice skating rinks for outdoor enthusiasts to enjoy the beauty of the snowy landscape.

7. Dog-friendly parks: Ottawa's dog-friendly parks provide a secure setting for dogs to run, play, and interact with other canine buddies for people who have furry pets.

8. Special occasions and festivals: Parks hold a variety of activities and festivals all year round, including cultural festivals, outdoor concerts, and movie evenings under the stars.

For visitors of all ages, Ottawa's parks and playgrounds provide a variety of activities. These green places serve as the backdrop for priceless experiences, whether you're looking for peace and quiet in the outdoors, enjoyable family vacations, or chances for outdoor activity. Discover the unending excitement and adventure Ottawa's parks and playgrounds contain for everyone by embracing their beauty and variety. So, prepare your picnic basket, don your walking shoes, and enjoy the great outdoors in the energetic capital of Canada.

Funhaven Entertainment Centre

Look no farther than Ottawa's Funhaven Entertainment Centre for an action-packed day of fun and entertainment. This enormous indoor amusement park is a refuge for groups of friends, families, and thrill-seekers of all ages, and it provides a wide range of events and attractions that ensure an amazing time. In the capital, Funhaven should be at the top of your list for enjoyable outings:

1. Thrilling Attractions: Funhaven offers a wide variety of exhilarating activities for visitors of all ages and interests. There is no lack of thrill and hilarity to be enjoyed, from heart-pounding laser tag bouts to exhilarating bumper cars.

2. Play these interactive arcade games: Enter the cutting-edge arcade to discover a wide range of interactive games and time-honoured favourites. It's a fun task for youngsters and adults to earn tickets and exchange them for interesting rewards.

3. Ropes course indoors: The indoor ropes course will put your agility and daring to the test if you're looking for an aerial experience. As you go at a great height, overcome your worries and negotiate difficult barriers.

4. Mini Golf Extravaganza: Immerse yourself in a fanciful world of mini-golf entertainment. You will experience thrilling twists and turns on the imaginatively planned course, which makes it a fun pastime for groups of friends and family.

5. Family-friendly restaurants: Recharge with delectable meals and beverages in the on-site restaurant after an eventful day. The extensive menu of the kid-friendly restaurant has something for every palate.

6. Birthday celebrations and group activities: A popular spot for group trips and birthday celebrations is Funhaven. With specialised hostesses, exclusive access to attractions, and

customised décor, the party packages guarantee an unforgettable celebration.

7. Safe and sanitary surroundings: Funhaven puts a priority on cleanliness and safety to make sure that guests may have fun without fear. All visitors will feel at home thanks to the facility's dedication to cleanliness and safety.

8. Special occasions and promotions: No matter the season, Funhaven is a fun destination to visit because of its year-round special events and promotions, which include themed evenings, holiday festivities, and reduced packages.

Everyone can look forward to a full day of nonstop entertainment at Funhaven Entertainment Centre. This bright indoor amusement park offers it all, whether you're a thrill-seeker, a gamer, or simply seeking to have a good time with family and friends. So, assemble your loved ones and set off on an exciting excursion to Funhaven, where you'll make priceless memories that you'll treasure long after the day is done. Prepare yourself for a world of adventure right in the centre of Ottawa!

OTTAWA'S CULINARY SCENE

Must-Try Canadian Dishes

The delicious variety of foods available in Canada's diversified culinary scene reflect the nation's rich cultural history and abundance of natural resources. These must-try Canadian meals are a feast of flavours from coast to coast that will leave your taste buds hankering for more:

1. poutine: The delectable meal poutine, a Canadian institution, hails from Quebec. It includes a bed of golden-brown French fries that have been covered in silky cheese curds and savoury gravy. Enjoy this rich, comforting dish that perfectly encapsulates Canadian cooking.

2. Butter Tarts: Butter tarts are delicious sweets with a flaky pastry shell and a rich interior composed of butter, sugar, and perhaps a touch of maple syrup or raisins. They are a well-known Canadian dish. They are a must-have for every sweet taste due to their enticing gooey centre.

3. Nanaimo bars: These no-bake bars, which bear the name of the Vancouver Island city of Nanaimo, are a treat for dessert lovers. A wonderful balance of

tastes and sensations is created by the layers of crumbly cookie foundation, creamy custard, and a rich chocolate topping.

4. Montreal-style Bagels: These are smaller, denser, and honey-sweetened in comparison to their New York counterparts. These chewy, hand-rolled, wood-fired bagels are often eaten with cream cheese or smoked salmon.

5. Tourtière: Tourtière is a savoury meal made with seasoned ground meat that is often a blend of beef, pig, and veal. It is a classic French-Canadian meat pie. During gatherings and festivities during the holidays, this substantial pie is a mainstay.

6. Bannock: A favourite among Native Americans, bannock is a simple yet filling bread that is usually prepared over an open flame using flour, baking soda, and water. Use savoury or sweet toppings or eat it alone.

7. Lobster roll: The lobster roll is a seaside delicacy that includes tender morsels of fresh lobster flesh placed on a buttered, toasted bread. A must-try while travelling to the Maritime provinces of Canada is this seafood delicacy.

8. Pure maple: syrup is a real Canadian treasure that is made from the sap of maple trees. For a genuine taste of Canada's maple trees, drizzle it over pancakes, waffles, or even ice cream.

9. A sandwich with peameal bacon: Peameal bacon sandwiches, a speciality of Toronto, include succulent pork loin that has been brined, rolled and dusted with cornmeal. This meaty sandwich is a Canadian favourite and is presented on soft bread.

10. Wild salmon: Some of the best wild salmon in the world may be found in the clear seas off the coast of Canada. Enjoy this juicy fish's rich, delicate flavour when it is served in a variety of ways, such as grilled fillets or smoked specialties.

Embrace Canada's culinary delights and set off on a culinary tour that showcases the nation's regional specialities and cultural history. Canadian food offers a remarkable and scrumptious experience that will leave you yearning for more of the delicious flavours of the True North, whether you're indulging in the indulgence of poutine, savouring the sweetness of butter tarts, or enjoying the freshness of wild salmon.

Local Food Markets

Local food markets in Ottawa provide a delicious tour of the area's varied culinary scene. These markets are a feast for the senses, offering everything from fresh fruit and handcrafted products to international flavours and sweet treats. Explore these local markets that you really must go to in order to experience Ottawa's lively and varied culinary culture:

1. ByWard Market: Offering a diverse selection of fresh produce, gourmet delicacies, handmade crafts, and foreign cuisine, the famous ByWard Market is a hive of activity. Explore the colourful booths, try the local cheeses, buy some fresh fruit, and take in the scent of the pastries that have just been prepared.

2. Market for Farmers in Ottawa: The Ottawa Farmers' Market, which is held in Lansdowne Park, is a paradise for foodies looking for artisanal goods and farm-fresh vegetables. Enjoy the satisfaction of making purchases directly from neighbourhood farmers, bakers, and craftsmen who take delight in their homemade goods.

3. Parkdale Market: In Ottawa's Hintonburg neighbourhood, Parkdale Market is a hidden treasure. It has been providing the neighbourhood for more than 90 years and is renowned for its extensive variety of fresh fruits, vegetables, and flowers. Don't pass up the opportunity to interact with local producers and take advantage of the seasonal bounty.

4. Farmers' Market in Carp: The Carp Farmers' Market is a wonderful rural respite only a short drive from Ottawa's downtown. Browse a broad selection of locally produced foods including fruits, vegetables, meats, cheeses, and baked items while taking in the warm environment.

5. Kanata Farmers' Market: This market, which is situated in the Kanata neighbourhood, provides a variety of fresh and organic vegetables as well as one-of-a-kind handcrafted goods. Discover handmade jewellery, taste home-made preserves, and listen to live music while perusing the market's products.

6. Rideau Centre Market: The Rideau Centre Market, which is conveniently located in the centre of downtown Ottawa, is a great place to get a quick snack or unusual gourmet goods. It is a foodie's

heaven since it offers a wide variety of foreign cuisine.

7. Cumberland Farmers' Market: This market, which brings together regional farmers and artists, is tucked away in the quaint town of Cumberland. Enjoy the welcoming atmosphere while shopping for fresh produce, honey, handcrafted items, and more.

8. Neighbourhood markets in Glebe: Seasonal markets like the Glebe Artisan Market and the Glebe Market are held in the thriving Glebe neighbourhood. These markets provide an outstanding selection of handmade goods, regional goods, and delectable snacks that reflect the local culture.

The local food markets in Ottawa are a veritable gold mine of culinary treats, providing a delicious mix of handcrafted products and fresh, locally sourced ingredients. By visiting these markets, you may meet the local food producers, enjoy the welcoming atmosphere of Ottawa's culinary scene, and learn about distinctive flavours. The city's food markets guarantee a fascinating and genuine experience that will give you a greater understanding of the region's gastronomic riches, whether you're a food connoisseur, a supporter of local enterprises, or just looking for a savoury adventure.

Fine Dining

The fine dining options available in Ottawa are many and appeal to people with discriminating tastes and those looking for an unforgettable dining experience. These upmarket restaurants are perfect for special events, celebrations, and decadent nights because they combine artistry, inventiveness, and great service. Here are a few of Ottawa's best fine dining establishments that guarantee an exceptional dining experience:

1. Atelier: Atelier is a Michelin-starred restaurant that elevates eating under the direction of famous Chef Marc Lepine. A multi-course culinary journey that fascinates and surprises customers with each dish is offered by Atelier, a restaurant renowned for its inventive tasting menu and molecular gastronomy methods.

2. Riviera: Riviera, which is housed in a gorgeously renovated historic structure, is opulent and sophisticated. Seasonal ingredients and flawless presentation are used throughout its menu to give a

new take on traditional French and Mediterranean cuisine.

3. Beckta Dining and Wine: A well-known restaurant, Beckta, focuses on modern Canadian cuisine with international influences. Dining at Beckta is a celebration of exquisite flavours and culinary talent, with an excellent wine list and a constantly-changing cuisine that emphasises local ingredients.

4. North & Navy: North & Navy is an Italian restaurant that emphasises the culinary traditions of Northern Italy. This restaurant gives a sophisticated taste of the regional delicacies of Italy, including house-made pasta and meals inspired by the Adriatic coast.

5. The Stofa Restaurant: Chef Jason Sawision's Stofa Restaurant serves up contemporary Canadian cuisine with a nod to international influences. The restaurant's innovative menus are a tribute to Chef Sawision's culinary prowess and love of fine ingredients.

6. Courtyard Restaurant: This magnificent fine dining venue is housed in the ByWard Market and is renowned for its warm environment and

traditional French cuisine. It provides a pleasant eating experience with its charming patio and historical surroundings.

7. The Wellington Gastropub: The Wellington Gastropub offers a broad variety of craft beers along with a mix of upscale gastropub food. The restaurant's always changing cuisine showcases the freshest seasonal and local foods, and the casual but chic ambiance enhances the whole eating experience.

8. Allium: A tiny and attractive restaurant called Allium provides a farm-to-table dining experience with an emphasis on organic products and sustainability. The culinary prowess of Chef Arup Jana is evident in meals that highlight the flavours of the season.

Talented chefs push the limits of flavour and presentation when it comes to fine dining in Ottawa. These fine dining venues encourage you to indulge in a world of culinary talent and savour the greatest flavours, from creative tasting menus to traditional French and Italian fare. These restaurants provide an evening of refinement, first-rate service, and a celebration of the best food Ottawa has to offer, whether you're celebrating a special event or just looking for an unforgettable dining experience.

Casual Eateries

The calm and pleasant ambience of Ottawa's casual restaurants makes them the perfect places to enjoy a tasty meal without the formality of fine dining. These casual restaurants in Ottawa will satisfy your cravings for fast bites, comfort cuisine, or flavours from across the world:

1. Art-Is-In Bakery: Locals love Art-Is-In Bakery because of its delicious pastries, handmade bread, and brunch options. For foodies, this bakery is a must-visit since it serves delicious baked products and exquisite sandwiches.

2. Pure Kitchen: The go-to place for delicious plant-based food is Pure Kitchen. The menu at this vegetarian and vegan restaurant is varied, with dishes including nutrient-dense bowls, inventive salads, and delectable plant-based burgers.

3. Hintonburger: Hintonburger is the place to go if you're in the mood for a traditional burger. This well-known burger restaurant offers

mouthwatering, juicy burgers with a selection of toppings.

4. Elgin Street Diner: Popular for comfort food at all hours of the day, the Elgin Street Diner is open twenty-four hours a day. Enjoy filling meals, diner favourites, and decadent milkshakes.

5. La Bottega Nicastro: A beautiful Italian deli and grocery shop, La Bottega Nicastro serves a variety of delicious sandwiches, crisp salads, and mouth watering pastries. It's the ideal location for a brief yet filling meal.

6. Zak's Diner: At Zak's restaurant, a retro-themed restaurant dishing up traditional comfort meals like burgers, milkshakes, and all-day breakfasts, go back in time.

7. Shawarma Palace: Shawarma Palace is a local favourite for anyone seeking flavours from the Middle East. You may be confident that their mouthwatering shawarma wraps and dishes will fulfil your cravings.

8. Green Rebel: A restaurant serving healthful bowls, sandwiches, and smoothies created with fresh ingredients is called Green Rebel.

9. La Pataterie Hulloise: At La Pataterie Hulloise, you may indulge in a variety of poutine concoctions topped with delectable toppings and experience a Canadian staple.

10. SuzyQ Doughnuts: SuzyQ Doughnuts is a must-go-to place for dessert or a sweet treat. Their mouthwatering doughnuts are delicious and available in a range of flavours.

The variety of flavours and culinary experiences offered by Ottawa's informal restaurants make them ideal for a quick snack or a leisurely supper with friends and family. These informal restaurants promise to satiate every appetite and provide a lovely sample of Ottawa's lively culinary scene. They offer everything from delectable sandwiches to comfort meals and exotic treats.

Pubs and Breweries

The vibrant and passionate environment that Ottawa's pubs and breweries provide makes them ideal places to savour a variety of craft brews, locally made ales, and mouthwatering pub grub. These pubs and breweries in Ottawa will give you a taste of the flourishing craft beer industry in the city, whether you're a beer connoisseur or simply looking for a fun night out:

1. Clocktower Brew Pub: Craft beer enthusiasts often visit Clocktower Brew Pub, which has many sites across Ottawa. They provide a selection of handmade beers, ranging from classic ales to avant-garde seasonal brews, all served in a warm and welcoming pub environment.

2. Beyond the Pale Brewing Company: This neighbourhood favourite is renowned for its inventive and daring artisan brews. They take great satisfaction in pushing the limits of brewing, producing distinctive and tasty beers that excite beer connoisseurs.

3. The Tooth and Nail Brewing Company: The beers produced by Tooth & Nail Brewing Company have a wide variety of flavours and new twists on classic brewing techniques. The roomy brewery taproom is a great spot to unwind with friends over a pint.

4. Flora Hall Brewing Company: Flora Hall Brewing, which is located in a stunning history building, provides a cosy and inviting atmosphere in which to savour artisan brews and a well chosen

menu of pub-inspired foods. Every time you go, a new and interesting experience is guaranteed by their constantly changing beer selection.

5. Lowertown Brewery: In the heart of Ottawa's ByWard Market, Lowertown Brewery offers a rustic-chic environment and a variety of handmade brews that go well with their mouthwatering food menu.

6. Dominion City Brewing Company: Dominion City Brewing Company is committed to making premium craft beers with an emphasis on utilising ingredients from local suppliers. They provide a comfortable setting in their taproom where you can enjoy their creative beers.

7. Waller Street Brewing: Small-batch brewery Waller St. Brewing takes pleasure in producing a diverse range of beers, from hop-forward IPAs to creamy stouts. Their tasting facility offers a cosy and welcoming atmosphere in which to savour their masterpieces.

8. Overflow Brewing Company: A brewery with a strong sense of community, Overflow Brewing Company offers a variety of small-batch brews.

Their taproom is a comfortable setting for socialising and sampling their most recent beers.

The bars and breweries in Ottawa are evidence of the city's thriving craft beer scene. These places provide a great chance to experience a variety of local beers while immersing yourself in Ottawa's vibrant pub culture, whether you're a beer lover or just seeking for a fun and exciting night out. Raise a glass in celebration of Ottawa's breweries and the craft beer revolution as you sip on everything from traditional ales to cutting-edge craft brews.

Craft Beer Scene

Ottawa's craft beer sector has experienced a remarkable transition, developing into a thriving neighbourhood of brewers that enthrals both beer experts and amateurs. Here are some reasons to check out the capital's craft beer scene:

1. Booming Brewery Scene: Ottawa is home to a thriving collection of craft brewers, each with its own unique personality and selection. The city's beer scene is constantly growing, promoting innovation and craftsmanship, with everything from cosy neighbourhood microbreweries to busy craft beer pioneers.

2. Collaboration: The craft beer scene in Ottawa is built on a collaborative spirit. Brewmasters from various breweries collaborate to produce singular and one-of-a-kind beers, establishing a feeling of community and a passion for superior brewing.

3. Seasonal & Experimental Brews: Ottawa's craft brewers continuously push the limits of brewing with their creative and audacious recipes. Every season, they release brand-new, experimental beers that surprise beer connoisseurs with their flavours and aromatic qualities.

4. Tasting Rooms & Taprooms: At the city's warm tasting rooms and taprooms, the experience of savouring craft beer is amplified. Visitors are encouraged to try a variety of brews, interact with the brewers, and get fully immersed in the love that goes into each pint.

5. Craft Beer Festivals: Ottawa holds a variety of craft beer festivals all year long, bringing brewers and beer lovers together in a celebration of hops and friendship. The best craft beers from both local and regional brewers are featured at these exciting events.

6. Emphasis on Local Ingredients: Many craft brewers in Ottawa value locally produced ingredients since they are committed to sustainability and have a passion for the area. These beers capture the flavour of the region's terroir via the use of speciality malts and hops that are cultivated nearby.

7. Sustainability and Community Involvement: Craft brewers in Ottawa value sustainability and community involvement and understand how important it is to protect the environment. They demonstrate a feeling of responsibility for their environment by actively engaging in sustainability practices and supporting neighbourhood concerns.

8. Beer & Food Pairings: Craft brewers and the local culinary industry in Ottawa often work together to create delicious beer and food matching experiences. These interactions produce flavour combinations that work well together, enhancing the pleasure of both beer and food.

Ottawa's craft beer culture is a vibrant and varied tapestry of artistry, camaraderie, and craftsmanship. Craft brewers in Ottawa have started a flavour revolution that thrills both residents and tourists thanks to their dedication to pushing the frontiers of flavour, collaborative spirit, and undying affection for the area. Take a trip to the heart and spirit of Ottawa's craft brewing sector by embracing the enthusiasm and innovation of the city's craft beer culture. Cheers to the capital's craft beer scene!

Iconic Pubs

There are several famous pubs in Ottawa, each with its own special charm and personality. These places have become cherished monuments and meeting places for both residents and tourists. Here are a few of Ottawa's most recognisable bars:

1. The Royal Oak: A well-known chain of bars with several sites around the city is called The Royal Oak. It provides a typical British pub experience, complete with substantial pub food, a large range of beers on tap, and a friendly environment.

2. D'Arcy McGee's Irish Pub: This Irish bar, named after Thomas D'Arcy McGee, one of Canada's Fathers of Confederation, honours its namesake with a welcoming Irish atmosphere. D'Arcy McGee's is a favourite hangout for both residents and visitors because it offers live music, traditional Irish food, and a variety of whiskies.

3. The Manx Tavern: The Manx Pub is a cherished neighbourhood landmark located in Ottawa's historic Glebe neighbourhood. This quaint pub is a locals' favourite hangout because of its extensive cuisine, specialty beer variety, and laid-back environment.

4. Heart & Crown Irish Pubs: The Heart & Crown Irish Pubs provide a genuine Irish pub experience and have many sites throughout Ottawa. It's a terrific location to unwind with a pint and some enjoyable company because of the live music, authentic Irish food, and the welcoming atmosphere.

5. The Lieutenant's Pump: Lieutenant's Pump is a historic bar with a long history going back to the 1980s that is situated in Ottawa's hip Glebe neighbourhood. It provides a wide range of craft beers and traditional pub fare in a pleasant and welcoming environment.

6. The Chateau Lafayette (The Laff): The Chateau Lafayette, often known as The Laff, has been a neighbourhood favourite since 1849 and is referred to as Ottawa's oldest pub. With its wooden décor,

live music, and wide range of drinks, it emanates a traditional pub ambiance.

7. Patty Boland's Irish Pub: The bustling Irish bar Patty Boland's is situated in the ByWard Market area of Ottawa. It offers a sizable whisky selection, live entertainment and food that is influenced by Irish and Canadian pub cuisine.

8. The Lieutenant's Pump: A cosy and welcoming ambiance can be found in "The Lieutenant's Pump," another famous bar in Ottawa's Hintonburg district. It's a terrific place to relax with friends while savouring a variety of drinks and pub fare.

Visitors may get a taste of the strong community spirit and rich pub culture of Ottawa by visiting these renowned pubs, which have become an essential part of the city's social fabric. These legendary pubs provide an exceptional experience in the city, whether you're wanting to unwind with friends, take in some live entertainment, or indulge in substantial pub grub.

SHOPPING IN OTTAWA

ByWard Market Shopping District

The ByWard Market is a popular and well-known retail area in Ottawa, known for its upbeat ambiance, wide variety of goods, and lengthy history. The market, which is located in the centre of town, is well-liked by both residents and visitors. What makes the ByWard Market a must-see is listed below:

1. Shopaholic Extravaganza: The ByWard Market, which has a variety of boutiques, specialised stores and artisanal businesses, is a shopper's delight. You'll discover a treasure trove of things to fit every taste and style, from cutting-edge fashion stores to one-of-a-kind craft and gift shops.

2. Fresh Foods and the Farmer's Market: The lively outdoor farmer's market, where local farmers and sellers offer fresh vegetables, flowers, baked goods, and handcrafted crafts, is one of the market's primary attractions. The greatest regional flavours and ingredients from Ottawa may be found there.

3. Gastronomic Delights: A wide variety of restaurants, cafés, and diners can be found at The

ByWard Market, which is a gastronomic paradise. It's the perfect place for food lovers since you can enjoy a variety of foreign cuisines and local delicacies, from fast food to fine dining.

4. Culture and the arts

The market is bursting with art and culture, and its streets are lined with galleries, studios, and cultural institutions. Visitors may peruse the creations of regional artists, go to exhibits, and experience the capital's thriving arts community.

5. Entertainment and Nightlife:

The ByWard Market comes to life as dusk falls with its exciting nightlife. For visitors looking for nighttime entertainment, the area provides a variety of pubs, clubs, and live music venues, providing a vibrant and exciting environment.

6. Historical Monuments: In addition to its modern products, the ByWard Market is home to a number of historic sites, including as the Notre-Dame Cathedral Basilica, a spectacular Gothic Revival cathedral that dominates the neighbourhood.

7. Events and festivals: The ByWard Market holds a variety of events and festivals all year long, from holiday festivities and culinary festivals to art

exhibits and musical performances. These activities increase the market's vibrant atmosphere and give visitors more reasons to go.

8. The Central Location: The ByWard Market's central position makes it readily accessible and a practical starting place for visiting Ottawa. It is situated close to important sights including Parliament Hill and the National Gallery of Canada.

The ByWard Market is a well-known and bustling retail area that exemplifies Ottawa's multicultural and eclectic culture. The market is a centre of activity and a must-visit location for anybody wishing to experience the heart and soul of the capital city with its lively farmer's market, unique retail choices, gastronomic pleasures, and rich history. The ByWard Market has something to offer every visitor, whether they're looking for one-of-a-kind retail bargains, mouth watering food, or a taste of Ottawa's cultural life.

Rideau Centre

In the centre of Ottawa, Ontario's downtown, sits the lively and well-known Rideau Centre. The shopping mall has established itself as a must-visit destination for both residents and visitors due to its wide variety of retailers, contemporary facilities, and convenient location. What makes Rideau Centre a shopping paradise is as follows:

1. Retail Paradise: Rideau Centre is home to nearly 180 retailers, providing a variety of alternatives for those who love fashion, technology, and home design. Shoppers may enjoy a shopping paradise that caters to a variety of interests and inclinations, from premium labels to well-known merchants.

2. Modern Ambiance: The facility received a significant remodelling that produced a modern and chic ambiance. The Rideau Centre offers consumers a stylish and welcoming atmosphere with its contemporary architecture and interior design.

3. Ideal Location: The Rideau Centre, which is ideally situated at the intersection of Rideau Street and Sussex Drive, is close to popular destinations including Parliament Hill and the ByWard Market. It is an easy stop for city visitors because of its accessibility.

4. Gastronomic Delights: The Rideau Centre provides a tempting selection of food choices in

addition to shopping. Visitors may take a pause and indulge in a wide variety of gastronomic pleasures, from fast eats to luxury eateries.

5. Indoor Comfort: The Rideau Centre offers a relaxing shopping environment, rain or shine. Its enclosed design protects guests from bad weather, delivering a pleasurable shopping experience all year round.

6. Activities and entertainment: The shopping experience is made more exciting by the centre's year-round hosting of numerous events and promotions. Additionally, guests eager to watch the newest movies have entertainment alternatives thanks to the complex's cutting-edge cinema theatre.

7. Guest Services and Amenities: Rideau Centre takes pride in its superior guest services, which include assisting and educating customers. Accessible facilities, kid-friendly play spaces, and family-friendly amenities all improve the entire shopping experience.

8. Initiatives for sustainability: The Rideau Centre is dedicated to environmental responsibility and sustainable practices. In order to lessen its carbon

impact and encourage sensible consumption, the institution concentrates on environmental activities.

The bustling retail culture in Ottawa is typified by Rideau Centre, which provides a wide variety of businesses, contemporary facilities, and a convenient location for both residents and tourists. The retail mall delivers an amazing shopping experience that captures the vibrant atmosphere of the nation's capital, from cutting-edge trends to mouthwatering culinary selections. The Rideau Centre continues to be a must-visit location that perfectly encapsulates the attraction of shopping in Ottawa, whether you're indulging in retail therapy, looking for entertainment, or just taking a walk through the centre of the city.

Sparks Street Mall

In the centre of Ottawa, Ontario's downtown, you'll find the historic Sparks Street Mall. Sparks Street has been a well-liked attraction for both residents and visitors due to its pleasant environment, cultural importance, and broad selection of stores and eateries. What makes Ottawa's Sparks Street Mall a must-see destination is listed below:

1. Rich History: Sparks Street has a rich history and is vital to Canadian history. With roots in the early 19th century, it is one of Canada's first pedestrian-only streets. Numerous historical events took place on this street, which has since developed into a thriving business district.

2. Pedestrian Paradise: Sparks Street is a pedestrian-only street that provides a comfortable and secure setting for leisurely walking, shopping, and eating. Visitors don't need to worry about driving as they leisurely explore the region.

3. Speciality stores and boutiques: A wide range of boutiques, specialised shops and lovely businesses can be found in Sparks Street Mall. Shoppers may find a treasure trove of one-of-a-kind treasures and gifts, ranging from regionally produced crafts to fashionable clothing.

4. Cafés and restaurants: The mall offers a large variety of restaurants, cafés, and diners, boasting a diversified culinary scene. Whether you're in the mood for foreign food or regional treats, Sparks Street offers selections to suit every taste.

5. Cultural Festivals and Events: Sparks Street often holds cultural events, live performances, and

festivals that enhance the lively ambiance. Visitors may take in outdoor performances, art displays, and holiday festivities.

6. Outdoor patios: A delightful outdoor dining experience and a buzzing social scene are produced on Sparks Street during the warmer months when many restaurants and coffee shops open their patios.

7. Public artwork and installations: Public art works, sculptures, and murals abound on Sparks Street, giving the pedestrian strip a creative flair. These pieces of art enhance the street's attractiveness and character.

8. The Central Location: The National War Memorial, Parliament Hill, and the Rideau Canal are all only a few steps away from the main attractions, making Sparks Street Mall a convenient starting point for visitors touring the city.

An iconic and historically important location that captures the essence of Ottawa's downtown is Sparks Street Mall. Its pedestrian-only setting, distinctive shops, delectable cuisine, and exciting cultural events make it a fascinating destination to discover and take in the heart and soul of the nation's capital. Sparks Street Mall provides an amazing experience that highlights the history and present beauty of Ottawa, whether you're taking a leisurely walk, exploring one-of-a-kind stores, or indulging in the regional cuisine.

Boutiques and Unique Shops

People looking for one-of-a-kind discoveries and locally crafted treasures will enjoy shopping in Ottawa's broad selection of boutiques and specialty stores. Here are some of the nicest locations to visit, which range from beautiful handmade shops to fashionable designer boutiques:

1. Boogie + Birdie: This store in the thriving Glebe neighbourhood sells a carefully picked range of goods manufactured in Canada, including clothing, accessories, home goods, and presents. Boogie & Birdie is renowned for emphasising local artisan support and promoting eco-friendly and sustainable goods.

2. Workshop Studio & Boutique, second:The Hintonburg business Workshop Studio & Boutique sells a variety of handmade items created by regional designers and artisans. Unique jewellery,

pottery, textiles, and other works of art may be found by visitors.

3. The boutique Viens Avec Moi: This chic store in the Westboro district offers a carefully chosen selection of attire, footwear, and accessories that are on-trend. The emphasis of the Viens Avec Moi Boutique is on current and elegant companies from Canada and beyond.

4. Maker House Company: Maker House Co. is a must-visit location for anyone looking for handcrafted items and locally manufactured products. This shop, which is situated in the thriving ByWard Market neighbourhood, provides a variety of goods made by over 100 Canadian craftsmen, including home décor, presents, and original artwork.

5. JV Studios: JV Studios is a distinctive store that sells modern and distinctive jewellery designs made by regional artist Jennifer Vachon. It is located in Wellington West. Her creations blend creativity and expertise to create unique standout pieces.

6. Goods Shop: In the Glebe district, Goods Shop offers a unique assortment of antique and contemporary furnishings, accessories, and home

décor. It is a gold mine for anyone trying to give their living spaces uniqueness and charm.

7. Flock Boutique: Located in the Wellington West neighbourhood, Flock Boutique has a carefully chosen collection of clothing and accessories from independent designers and Canadian brands. It is a destination for fashion-conscious people seeking distinctive and fashionable items.

8. The Village Quire: The Village Quire in Westboro is a hidden treasure for stationery lovers. This shop sells a variety of writing instruments, greeting cards, presents, and handcrafted items that honour the writing and gift-giving arts.

The boutiques and one-of-a-kind stores in Ottawa are a testament to the city's innovative spirit and dedication to promoting regional designers and artists. These shops provide an unmatched shopping experience with a hint of Ottawa's special character, whether you're looking for chic home décor, artisan jewellery, or fashion-forward apparel. You will undoubtedly find lovely and unique gifts that represent the city's thriving arts and crafts scene by exploring these hidden jewels.

Souvenir Ideas

You should get souvenirs from Ottawa that perfectly express the spirit of the city and its distinctive culture. Here are some suggestions for memorable travel memories as souvenirs:

1. Maple syrup, to start: A bottle of genuine Canadian maple syrup is a delectable and time-honoured gift since Canada is known for its maple syrup.

2. Inukshuk sculptures Inuit people of Northern Canada utilise inukshuks as stone markers. Figurines of inukshuks are meaningful and aesthetically pleasing gifts.

3. Merchandise bearing the Canadian Maple Leaf: Look for products like t-shirts, caps, mugs, or keychains that showcase the recognisable red maple leaf.

4. Souvenirs with moose and beaver themes are popular selections, ranging from cuddly toys to mugs and representing Canadian nature.

5. Postcards and prints with an Ottawa theme: Purchase prints or postcards of recognisable Ottawa

sights like Parliament Hill, the Rideau Canal, or the Peace Tower to take home.

6. Hockey memorabilia: Ottawa has a vibrant hockey culture, and hockey is a cherished sport in Canada. Think about purchasing mementos from hockey games, such as pucks, jerseys, or keychains.

7. Canadian whisky: Canada is renowned for producing whisky. A bottle of Canadian whisky makes a great present for loved ones.

8. Handmade crafts manufactured by artisans Shops and local markets are good places to find handcrafted goods and artisanal crafts. These could include ceramics, jewellery, textiles, and works of art created by regional artists.

9. Books and City Guides for Ottawa To learn more about the city and nation, get a guidebook to Ottawa or a book about Canadian history and culture.

10. Souvenirs in the shape of a maple leaf These mementos, which include magnets and biscuits in the shape of maple leaves, are entertaining and characteristic of Canada.

11. Consider purchasing genuine Indigenous artwork, crafts, or jewellery to support the First Nations, Métis, and Inuit peoples' unique cultural heritage.

12. Merchandise with the Canadian Flag: Look for trinkets like scarves, patches, or buttons that feature the pattern of the Canadian flag.

13. Local treats and food: Bring some locally produced Canadian goodies like Nanaimo bars, butter tarts, or chocolates home.

Keep in mind to select mementos that are meaningful to you personally and that match your preferences and hobbies. These souvenirs will serve as a memory of your time in Ottawa and will enhance the value of your recollections.

NIGHTLIFE AND ENTERTAINMENT

Live Music Venues

Ottawa has a thriving live music scene, with several venues that cater to various musical styles and tastes. The city has lots to offer whether you like rock, jazz, folk, or electronic music. Here are a few of Ottawa's well-liked live music venues:

1. Bluesfest at LeBreton Flats: One of the biggest music events in Canada, Ottawa Bluesfest draws talented musicians from a variety of genres. It takes place in July and features a diverse range of performers on many stages.

2. The National Arts Centre (NAC) The NAC presents a wide variety of live events, including jazz jam sessions, classical music concerts, performances by contemporary artists, and more. It is the perfect location for music lovers because of its exceptional acoustics.

3. The Bronson Centre: The Bronson Centre is a multi-use location where live music performances, events, and concerts take place. It supports a range of musical styles, including punk, metal, and independent and alternative.

4. Maverick's Bar: Live music events are often held at Mavericks, particularly rock, punk, and metal concerts. It is renowned for its cosy atmosphere, which enables fans to interact closely with the musicians.

5. The Rainbow Restaurant In Ottawa, live music is often performed at this historic location. Its warm, intimate atmosphere makes it a favourite among fans of blues, jazz, and rock.

6. Irene's Pub: The popular neighbourhood venue Irene's has live music virtually every evening. It is renowned for its welcoming environment and offers a variety of musical styles, including folk, country, and indie.

7. The TARG House: Live music, vintage arcade games, and perogies are all combined at House of TARG to provide a distinctive and enjoyable experience. There are a variety of punk, rock, and metal bands on it.

8. Live! on Elgin: This facility presents showcases, open mic nights, and live music events to benefit local artists. It's a terrific location to find

up-and-coming artists and take in live performances in a cosy atmosphere.

9. Theatre at Algonquin Commons: This theatre, which is a part of Algonquin College, presents a variety of live music concerts, comedies, and other plays.

10. Mercury Lounge: Popular venues for electronic, dance, and DJ acts include Mercury Lounge. It has a dance floor and a fun ambiance that's perfect for late-night entertainment.

Ottawa's live music venues cater to a wide clientele, so whether you enjoy large music festivals, cosy bars, or small concert halls, it's a place where music fans can discover their ideal rhythm.

Clubs and Bars

There are several clubs and pubs in Ottawa where you can go out dancing, listening to live music, and mingling. Here are a few of the city's well-liked pubs and clubs:

1. The Bourbon Room: The Bourbon Room has a variety of rock, metal, and alternative bands and is renowned for its vivacious environment and live

music. For people who like bustling crowds and live entertainment, it's a terrific location.

2. Barrymore's Music Hall: A historical location, Barrymore's organises themed parties, DJ nights, and live music events. It's a well-liked location for dancing and listening to many musical genres.

3. Alcohol Retail Party Bar: This distinctive pub has a dance floor, retro-themed furnishings and old-school video games. Young party goers seeking a lighthearted and enjoyable environment love it.

4. Zaphod Beeblebrox: Zaphod Beeblebrox, a storied club in Ottawa, is well-known for its varied selection of music, which includes indie, rock, and techno. It has a varied schedule of themed evenings and live acts.

5. The Lookout Bar: The Lookout Bar in the ByWard Market provides a variety of live music, DJ performances and karaoke evenings.

6. Lowertown Brewery: Craft brewery Lowertown Brewery has frequent live music events and a fun environment. It's a fantastic location for sipping on regional craft beer and taking in some top-notch music.

7. The Moscow Tea Room: This chic pub provides a distinctive and upmarket experience that is reminiscent of Moscow in the 1950s. It offers a wide variety of beverages, and live music creates the perfect atmosphere for a stylish evening out.

8. The Crazy Horse Stonegrill Steakhouse & Saloon is located at: The Crazy Horse is a well-known country-themed pub that features line dancing, live country music and a vibrant Western ambiance.

9. Nightclub Maison: Modern nightclub Maison has many levels and dance floors where DJs play electronic, dance, and Top 40 music.

10. Irish pubs Heart & Crown: Heart & Crown provides a vibrant Irish pub experience at its several locations, complete with live music, authentic Irish food, and a warm atmosphere.

Please be aware that depending on the day of the week and the season, Ottawa's nightlife scene may change. Before making plans for your night out, it's also a good idea to verify the schedule and age limits for each place.

Theatre and Performing Arts

Ottawa boasts a robust theatrical and performing arts community, with plays and performances to suit all interests. The city has various facilities that appeal to performing arts fans, ranging from world-class theatrical shows to contemporary dance and live music concerts. Here are some important locations and organisations to investigate:

1. National Arts Centre: The National Arts Centre is one of Canada's major performing arts facilities, offering a diverse spectrum of acts such as theatre, dance, classical music, and contemporary productions. It has three stages: the large Southam Hall, the tiny Azrieli Studio, and the Fourth Stage, which is used for more experimental performances.

2. Great Canadian theatrical group (GCTC):The Great Canadian Theatre Company (GCTC) is a professional theatrical group that highlights Canadian works and writers. It provides plays that are thought-provoking and socially relevant to the Canadian experience.

3. Shenkman Arts Centre: The Shenkman Arts Centre, located on the city's eastern outskirts, is a multi-disciplinary venue that offers a variety of

performing arts events, including theatrical shows, dance performances, and concerts.

4. The Gladstone Theatre: The Gladstone theatrical in Ottawa is a historic facility that hosts a variety of theatrical plays, including dramas, comedies, and musicals by local and visiting theatre groups.

5. The Arts Court Theatre: Arts Court Theatre, located in the centre of the ByWard Market, is a multipurpose performance facility that presents a variety of performing arts activities, including theatre, dance, and music.

6. Orpheus Musical Theatre Society: Orpheus is a community-based musical theatre group that performs Broadway-style musicals and shows in a variety of Ottawa locations.

7. The Odyssey Theatre: Odyssey Theatre specialises in physical theatre and produces unique and interesting shows in Strathcona Park throughout the summer.

8. Ballet and Dance Companies: Several ballet and dance organisations, including the National Ballet of Canada, the Ottawa Ballet, and the Greta

Leeming Studio of Dance, perform in Ottawa throughout the year.

9. The Little Theatre of Ottawa: Ottawa Little Theatre, one of Canada's oldest community theatres, produces a wide range of plays, from classics to modern pieces.

10. Fringe Festival of Ottawa: The Ottawa Fringe Festival is held every year and features a wide programme of independent theatrical works by local, national, and international artists.

Whether you're a theatre buff or just looking for a fun night out, Ottawa's theatre and performing arts industry provides something for everyone, featuring both local and international talent.

Festivals and Events

Ottawa is a city that likes to celebrate, and it holds a variety of festivals and events throughout the year that highlight its cultural diversity, talent, and community spirit. Here are some of Ottawa's most popular festivals and events:

1. Winter Interlude: Winterlude, held in February, is one of Ottawa's most well-known celebrations.

Winter is celebrated with ice sculptures, skating on the frozen Rideau Canal (the world's biggest skating rink), and other winter sports.

2. Celebrations for Canada Day: Canada's national day is commemorated on July 1st with a variety of activities, including concerts, parades, fireworks, and ceremonies on Parliament Hill.

3. Tulip Festival in Ottawa: During the annual Tulip Festival in May, the city comes alive with colourful tulips. It honours the Dutch royal family's donation of 100,000 tulip bulbs to Canada during World War II.

4. Ottawa International Jazz Festival: This event, held in June, brings together world-class jazz artists for concerts, seminars, and outdoor performances.

5. The RBC Ottawa Bluesfest: The Bluesfest, which takes place in July, is one of North America's major music events, with a broad roster of performers and bands from many genres.

6. Canadian Tulip Festival: is held in the spring. This event, held in May as well, celebrates the beauty of tulips at a variety of venues across the city, including Commissioners Park.

7. Fringe Festival of Ottawa: The Ottawa Fringe Festival takes place in June and features independent theatrical works by local and international artists in a variety of locations around the city.

8. Christmas Lights in Canada: During the holiday season, Ottawa is decked up in festive lights, including a lighting ceremony on Parliament Hill.

9. The Ottawa International Animation Festival (OIAF):The OIAF is North America's biggest animation festival, showcasing a diverse selection of animated films from throughout the globe.

10. Dragon Boat Festival in Ottawa: During this annual event in June, the Ottawa River comes alive with dragon boat racing, music, and cultural activities.

10. Ottawa Chamberfest: This July classical music event features chamber music concerts by local and international musicians.

11. Ottawa International Writers Festival: This literary event features readings, debates, and book signings by well-known writers.

These are just a handful of the numerous festivals and events held in Ottawa throughout the year. Whatever time of year you come, there will almost certainly be a festival or event to attend, making your vacation to the nation's capital even more memorable and exciting.

Ottawa Bluesfest

The Ottawa Bluesfest is one of Canada's most well-known music events, recognised for its broad roster of performers and lively celebration of blues, rock, pop, and other music genres. Here's all you need to know about this legendary event:

1. Background and Location: The inaugural Ottawa Bluesfest, sometimes known simply as Bluesfest, was held in 1994. It is held every year in July and lasts 10 days. The event is hosted in LeBreton Flats, a picturesque outdoor site near the Canadian War Museum just west of Ottawa's central centre.

2. Performers and Music: Bluesfest welcomes a diverse spectrum of musical genre performers. While the festival's origins are in blues music, the programme has extended to include rock, pop, hip-hop, country, folk, and other genres. Bluesfest

has welcomed notable performers such as Bob Dylan, Foo Fighters, Lady Gaga, The Rolling Stones, and many more foreign and Canadian bands throughout the years.

3. Diverse Programming and Multiple Stages: The event comprises many stages, each of which hosts acts at the same time. As a result, audiences may enjoy a variety of musical performances throughout the day. Bluesfest provides a broad and inclusive musical experience, with big-name headliners on the main stage and new performers on smaller stages.

4. Food and Beverage Selections: Aside from the music, Bluesfest has a variety of food and beverage vendors serving a variety of gastronomic pleasures, including local and foreign cuisines. Festival Goers may eat tasty food while listening to music.

5. Involvement in the Community: Bluesfest contributes to the community through sponsoring local musicians and philanthropic causes. It serves as a platform for local artists while also giving back to the community via different programmes and collaborations.

6. Efforts to Promote Sustainability: Bluesfest is devoted to environmental and sustainability activities. It has taken environmental initiatives such as trash reduction and recycling programmes to lessen its environmental effect.

7. Attendance and Tickets: Tickets for Ottawa Bluesfest may be bought in advance, and multiple ticket options, including single-day tickets and full festival packages, are available. The event draws a broad gathering of music fans from all across Ottawa and beyond.

The Ottawa Bluesfest is a summer highlight in the city, providing an outstanding music experience with a broad roster of musicians and a dynamic environment. The festival's dedication to presenting excellent performers from diverse genres, as well as its donations to the local community, have helped to make it a well-known event that draws people together in the spirit of music and joy. Bluesfest guarantees an amazing experience in the heart of Canada's capital city, whether you're a blues lover or just like fine music.

Winterlude

Winterlude is an annual winter celebration hosted in Ottawa that celebrates the beauty and charm of the season. It takes place over three weekends in February and attracts guests from all around the world. Here's all you need to know about this well-known festival:

1. Winter Wonderland: Winterlude celebrates the winter wonderland that Ottawa transforms into during this time of year. To create a spectacular winter experience, the event takes use of the city's snowy scenery, frozen rivers, and frigid weather.

2. How to Skate on the Rideau Canal: Skating on the Rideau Canal, which transforms into the world's biggest skating rink during the festival, is one of the festival's primary attractions. Visitors may glide down the canal's 7.8 kilometres (4.8 miles), going through downtown Ottawa and enjoying scenic sights along the way.

3. Amazing Ice Sculptures: The International Ice Sculpture Competition is another memorable aspect of Winterlude. Artists from all around the globe go to Ottawa to convert slabs of ice into complex and breathtaking sculptures. These ice

sculptures may be seen in numerous places across the city.

4. Snowflake Kingdom: Snowflake Kingdom, situated in Gatineau's Jacques-Cartier Park, is a family-friendly portion of Winterlude that has snow slides, snow sculptures, and a variety of outdoor activities for both children and adults.

5. Cultural Festivals: Winterlude showcases numerous ethnic performances, activities, and gastronomic experiences to highlight Canada's cultural variety. Visitors may enjoy music, dancing, and traditional arts & crafts from other nations.

6. Entertainment and Music: There will be live music performances, interactive entertainment, and creative exhibits throughout the festival, contributing to the festive environment and creating a dynamic scene for guests.

7. Hot Cocoa with BeaverTails: A trip to Winterlude would not be complete without sipping a cup of hot chocolate and indulging in BeaverTails, a popular Canadian delight. These delectable pastries in the form of a beaver's tail are often covered with sweet toppings such as chocolate, cinnamon, and maple syrup.

8. Evening Activities and Fireworks: The event culminates with stunning fireworks displays that light up the winter sky above the city, delivering a beautiful conclusion to the festivities. Throughout the festival, several nighttime events and activities keep the winter mood alive after the sun goes down.

Winterlude is a beloved winter celebration in Ottawa that delivers pleasure, excitement, and a feeling of community. The event provides an exquisite winter experience for residents and tourists alike, with its outdoor skating, spectacular ice sculptures, cultural festivities, and family-friendly activities. Winterlude is the ideal occasion to experience everything that winter has to offer in Canada's capital city, whether you're a winter aficionado or simply seeking to embrace the romance of the season.

SPORTS AND OUTDOOR ACTIVITIES

Ice Skating and Hockey

Ice skating and hockey are two prominent winter pastimes that are strongly embedded in the culture and lifestyle of Ottawa. The city's chilly winters and frozen rivers make these popular sports ideal. More information about ice skating and hockey in Ottawa may be found here:

1. Skating along the Rideau Canal: The Rideau Canal, a UNESCO World Heritage Site, is transformed into the world's biggest skating rink during the winter months. Locals and travellers alike rush to the canal to enjoy the one-of-a-kind experience of gliding over the frozen river, which offers breathtaking views of Parliament Hill and the city skyline.

2. Skating Rinks in the Open Air: Aside from the Rideau Canal, Ottawa has various outdoor skating rinks located across the city. Popular ones include City Hall's Rink of Dreams, Lansdowne Park Skating Court, and Parliament Hill's Sens Rink of Dreams.

3. Skating Rinks Indoors: For those who prefer indoor ice skating, there are several rinks at community centres, sports complexes, and arenas across Ottawa. These rinks are open all year, offering skaters of all ages and ability levels a pleasant and safe environment.

4. Recreational Hockey: Hockey is a defining Canadian sport, and inhabitants of Ottawa are devoted fans. Many small towns have outdoor rinks where neighbours come to play pick-up games, fostering companionship and community spirit.

5. Ottawa Senators of the National Hockey League: The Ottawa Senators play in the National Hockey League (NHL) and are the city's professional hockey club. Their home games are held at the Canadian Tyre Centre in Kanata, an Ottawa suburb. Attending a Senators game is a thrilling experience for hockey lovers and a fantastic opportunity to get immersed in the local sports culture.

6. Minor Hockey Leagues: Ottawa has a robust minor hockey scene, with various youth and amateur leagues allowing young players to hone their abilities and develop a passion for the game.

7. Sledge Hockey: The Ottawa Sledgehammers, a sledge hockey club that allows those with physical limitations to engage in the sport, are also based in Ottawa.

8. Skate-Learn Programmes: Ottawa has a variety of learn-to-skate programmes and hockey clinics for persons of all ages who are new to skating or hockey. These programmes are meant to help beginners improve their skating abilities and confidence.

Ice skating and hockey are important parts of Ottawa's winter character. These activities bring people together, establishing a feeling of community and a passion for winter sports. They range from gliding on the frozen Rideau Canal to cheering on the Ottawa Senators at the Canadian Tyre Centre. Whether you're an expert skater or a novice eager to try something new, Ottawa has a plethora of options to enjoy the winter enchantment of ice skating and hockey.

Cycling and Biking Trails

Ottawa is a bike-friendly city with an extensive network of riding and bicycling routes for bikers of all skill levels. There are several possibilities for riding aficionados, ranging from gorgeous routes along the Rideau Canal to off-road tracks through lush parks. Here are some of Ottawa's most popular riding and bike trails:

1. Rideau Canal Eastern Pathway: The Rideau Canal footpath runs beside the magnificent Rideau Canal, providing cyclists with a great route to explore. The eastern section of the route connects downtown Ottawa to the Ottawa Locks at Rideau Falls, offering scenic vistas of the canal and historic monuments.

2. Rideau River Western Pathway: This trail follows the Rideau River, taking bicycles from Mooney's Bay Park to the Canadian War Museum. The path winds past parks and natural fields, providing for a pleasant and restful ride.

3. Pathway along the Ottawa River: The Ottawa River Pathway is a picturesque walkway that travels along the Ottawa River and provides access to parks and beaches. It links to other paths and enables bicycles to go across the city.

4. Sir John A. Macdonald Parkway: This gorgeous parkway runs alongside to the Ottawa River and has a dedicated bike lane as well as stunning views of the river and the Gatineau Hills.

5. Experimental Farm Pathway: The Experimental Farm Pathway offers a serene ride through the Central Experimental Farm, a sprawling agricultural research site. Cyclists may enjoy the farm's gardens and fields as well as the open natural areas.

6. Ottawa River Pathway (Gatineau, Quebec):The Ottawa River Pathway continues across the river in Gatineau, Quebec, allowing a lovely ride through Gatineau Park and along the Quebec side of the river.

7. Greenbelt Pathways: The Greenbelt in Ottawa is a network of trails that weave through woods and meadows, providing picturesque and off-road riding opportunities.

8. Kanata Beaver Pond Trail: This path, located near Kanata, offers bikers on a picturesque journey via a beaver pond and wetland region, with potential for animal observations.

9. Trans Canada Trail (The Great Trail): The Trans Canada Trail, commonly known as The Great Trail, runs through Ottawa, providing long-distance riding alternatives for those seeking to go outside of the city.

10. NCC Bike Lanes: The National Capital Commission (NCC) maintains a number of bike lanes and walkways across Ottawa, ensuring that cyclists have safe and well-maintained routes.

Ottawa is a terrific city for cyclists to explore and enjoy the beauty of natural and urban environments, thanks to its large network of riding and bike routes. Whether you're a leisurely rider or a more daring biker, these paths provide a wide range of experiences to suit any riding enthusiast.

Skiing and Snowboarding

The closeness of Ottawa to the Gatineau Hills and the Laurentian Mountains gives sufficient chances for skiers and snowboarders to enjoy winter sports. While Ottawa is not a ski destination, there are numerous ski slopes within a comfortable driving distance. Here are a few popular ski and snowboarding spots around Ottawa:

1. Mont Tremblant: Mont Tremblant, located about two hours north of Ottawa, is one of the most well-known ski resorts in Eastern Canada. It has a large ski resort with a variety of slopes for all skill levels, as well as a picturesque pedestrian town with stores, restaurants, and après-ski activities.

2. Fortune Camp: Camp Fortune is a local favourite for skiing and snowboarding and is just a 20-minute drive from downtown Ottawa. It has a variety of terrain parks and slopes for beginners, intermediates, and experienced skiers.

3. Edelweiss Valley: Located about a 30-minute drive from Ottawa, Edelweiss Valley is a family-friendly ski resort with well-groomed slopes and a laid-back ambience that is great for novices and families.

4. Vorlage: Vorlage, located in the lovely hamlet of Wakefield, Quebec, is a modest ski resort recognised for its friendly feel and low prices. It's an excellent day excursion from Ottawa.

5. Calabogie Peaks Resort: Calabogie Peaks, about an hour's drive from Ottawa, has a gorgeous environment and an excellent choice of paths for

skiing and snowboarding, as well as other winter sports.

6. Mount Pakenham: Mount Pakenham, located approximately 45 minutes from Ottawa, is a family-friendly ski resort featuring a ski school and a terrain park for snowboarders.

7. Mountain Cascades: Mont Cascades, located in the Gatineau area, provides skiing and snowboarding possibilities within a short drive from Ottawa. It's a popular option among families and first-timers.

8. Mont Ste-Marie: Mont Ste-Marie, about an hour's drive from Ottawa, has a range of ski and snowboard courses as well as spectacular views of the surrounding region.

9. Sommet Edelweiss: Sommet Edelweiss, another choice in the Gatineau Hills, is a family-friendly ski resort with a variety of slopes ideal for all ability levels.

10. Mont Chilly: Mont Chilly, located in the Laurentian Mountains, provides a more private and leisurely skiing experience, ideal for skiers seeking a quieter ambiance.

These ski resorts near Ottawa provide a number of alternatives for winter sports fans to experience the excitement of skiing and snowboarding throughout the snowy season, whether you're a seasoned skier or a novice ready to hit the slopes.

Water Sports on the Ottawa River

During the summer months, the Ottawa River serves as a terrific playground for water sports lovers, with a variety of activities accessible to both residents and tourists. Here are several popular water sports activities on the Ottawa River, ranging from intense whitewater excursions to peaceful paddling:

1. Rafting on Whitewater: The Ottawa River is well-known for its thrilling whitewater rafting. There are parts for everyone, ranging from calm rapids for novices to more severe rapids for expert paddlers. Several organisations provide guided rafting trips with skilled instructors, making it an exciting and risk-free activity.

2. Canoeing and Kayaking: The Ottawa River's tranquil portions are ideal for kayaking and canoeing. Paddling along the calm waterways

enables you to take in the beauty, observe animals, and have a relaxing day. To explore the river, you may hire kayaks and canoes or join guided trips.

3. Stand-Up Paddleboarding(SUP): SUP is a popular river sport that allows you to explore the water while standing on a paddleboard. SUP rentals and instruction are provided for both inexperienced and seasoned paddlers.

4. Jet Boating: Jet boating experiences on the Ottawa River are offered for those looking for an adrenaline rush. These strong boats whisk riders away at great speeds, complete with exhilarating twists and splashes.

5. Waterskiing and wakeboarding: The Ottawa River's large parts provide plenty of area for wakeboarding and waterskiing. These water activities are offered at many spots along the river, and equipment rentals and instruction are often provided.

6. Fishing: The Ottawa River is home to a variety of fish species, making it an ideal location for anglers. You may fish from the riverbanks or from a boat to catch bass, pike, walleye, and other species.

7. Swimming: Many folks use the beaches and swimming spots along the Ottawa River to cool down and relax on hot summer days.

8. Sailing: If you like sailing, you may go sailing on the Ottawa River. The broad areas of the river give ideal sailing conditions.

9. River Surfing: River surfing is becoming more popular in certain areas, notably the Champlain Bridge Wave. Experienced surfers may catch and ride the standing wave formed by the strong currents in the city centre.

10. Scenic Cruises: Consider taking a picturesque cruise down the Ottawa River if you want a more relaxed experience. A number of boat companies provide sightseeing tours, supper cruises, and sunset excursions.

The numerous water sports activities on the Ottawa River make it a lively and pleasant location for outdoor lovers of all ability levels. The river provides something for everyone, whether you're looking for exhilarating experiences or a quiet day on the water.

Golf Courses

Ottawa has a wide range of golf courses to suit players of all ability levels. Here are some of the most popular golfing sites in the Ottawa region, ranging from gorgeous public courses to exclusive clubs:

1. Canadian Golf & Country Club: This 27-hole golf course, located just outside of Ottawa in Ashton, Ontario, provides a gorgeous location with rolling hills and breathtaking vistas. It's an open course that offers a hard but fun experience.

2. The Marshes Golf Club: The Marshes Golf Club, located in Ottawa's Kanata neighbourhood, is noted for its gorgeous and well-maintained 18-hole course. The course features natural wetlands, providing a one-of-a-kind golfing experience.

3. Eagle Creek Golf Club: Eagle Creek Golf Club, located in Dunrobin, Ontario, includes an 18-hole course tucked beside the Ottawa River. The course layout utilises the natural topography to provide a demanding and picturesque golfing experience.

4. Gatineau Golf and Country Club: This private golf club in Gatineau, Quebec, features a well-kept 18-hole course with a warm and inviting ambiance.

5. Hautes Plaines Golf Club: Hautes Plaines Golf Club, also in Gatineau, is an 18-hole course recognised for its natural beauty and demanding design.

6. Outaouais Golf Club: This public golf course in Rockland, Ontario, has 36 holes and allows players to pick from several course combinations.

7. Manderley on the Green: Manderley on the Green, located in North Gower, Ontario, provides a picturesque 27-hole course with spectacular vistas and a welcoming atmosphere.

8. Emerald Links Golf & Country Club: Emerald Links, located in Greely, Ontario, has an 18-hole championship course surrounded by natural beauty and wetlands.

9. Royal Ottawa Golf Club: The Royal Ottawa Golf Club, founded in 1891, is one of Canada's oldest golf clubs. It's a private club in Gatineau with a famous heritage and a traditional golfing experience.

10. Kanata Golf & Country Club: This Kanata private golf club provides a highly-regarded 18-hole

course as well as a variety of facilities to its members.

These are just a handful of the golf courses in and around Ottawa. Whether you're a seasoned golfer or just starting out, these courses provide a variety of settings and obstacles to fit your tastes and ability level. Remember that certain courses may need advanced booking or membership, so check with the particular clubs for availability and reservations.

DAY TRIPS FROM OTTAWA

Kingston

Kingston is a historic city in Eastern Ontario, Canada, on Lake Ontario's eastern shore. It boasts a rich legacy as one of Canada's oldest cities and is noted for its attractive waterfront, historic landmarks, and dynamic culture. The following are some of the important qualities and attractions that make Kingston a famous tourist destination:

1. Downtown Historic District: The downtown district of Kingston is rich with lovely old buildings and pleasant streets. It's a pedestrian-friendly neighbourhood with a variety of stores, restaurants, and cafés, making it a fun spot to walk about.

2. Kingston Waterfront: The coastline of the city along Lake Ontario provides spectacular vistas and a gorgeous environment. Visitors may take a walk along the waterfront, participate in outdoor activities, or take a picturesque boat excursion to see the city from the sea.

3. National Historic Site of Fort Henry: This UNESCO World Heritage Site provides interactive

tours and demonstrations that provide tourists with an insight into Canada's military history.

4. Kingston City Hall: With its stunning building and clock tower, Kingston City Hall is a major landmark in the downtown area.

5. Queen's University: Kingston is a university town, and Queen's University is a famous school noted for its academic brilliance and beautiful campus.

6. Kingston Penitentiary: This former maximum-security prison is now a national historic monument, and visitors may take guided tours to learn about the facility's history and renowned prisoners.

7. Kingston Thousand Islands Cruises: Kingston serves as the entry point to the Thousand Islands area, and boat trips leaving from the city provide a magnificent voyage across the lovely archipelago.

8. Market Square: Market Square, located in downtown Kingston, is a popular meeting place with seasonal farmers' markets, live music, and outdoor events.

9. National Historic Site of Bellevue House: This historic property, which was originally Sir John A. Macdonald's residence, provides guided tours and insights into his life.

10. Wolfe Island: A short boat trip from downtown Kingston, Wolfe Island offers a calm rural vacation complete with bike trails, lovely beaches, and breathtaking sunsets.

11. Kingston Pen Tours: Visitors may take guided tours of the Kingston Penitentiary, which provide an intriguing view into the history and operations of the old prison.

12. The Penitentiary Museum of Canada: This museum highlights artefacts and exhibits relating to the country's correctional system for individuals interested in the history of corrections in Canada.

Kingston's distinct combination of history, culture, and natural beauty makes it a popular tourist and residential destination. Kingston offers something for everyone, whether you want to explore its historic buildings, enjoy the shoreline, or experience the busy downtown atmosphere.

Mont Tremblant

Mont Tremblant is a prominent vacation town in Quebec, Canada's Laurentian Mountains. It is well-known for its breathtaking natural beauty, outdoor recreational opportunities, and lively village culture. Here are some of the main features and attractions that make Mont Tremblant such a popular destination:

1. Mont Tremblant Ski Resort: Mont Tremblant Ski Resort is one of North America's best ski resorts. It has a broad choice of slopes for all abilities of skiers and snowboarders, as well as great amenities, snowmaking, and a busy après-ski scene.

2. Mont Tremblant Village: This is a pedestrian-only area. Mont Tremblant community is a lovely European-style community located at the mountain's foot. It has cobblestone streets, colourful buildings, boutique stores, restaurants, and cafés, all of which contribute to the dynamic and beautiful atmosphere.

3. Tremblant Beach and Lake Activities: During the summer, guests may relax at Tremblant Beach, which is located beside Lake Tremblant. Swimming, paddleboarding, kayaking, and other water sports are available at the lake.

4. National Park of Mont-Tremblant: Mont-Tremblant National Park, located nearby, provides a wide wilderness region for hiking, camping, and exploration. The park has stunning landscapes, tranquil lakes, and a diverse range of species.

5. Golf Courses: Mont Tremblant is a golfer's dream, with many championship courses located within the scenic Laurentian Mountains.

6. Tremblant Casino: The Casino de Mont-Tremblant is a vibrant entertainment destination with gaming tables, slot machines, live concerts, and eating options.

7. Tremblant International Blues Festival: This yearly music event attracts prominent blues performers to the area and is popular among music fans.

8. Scenic Gondola Rides: The Panoramic Gondola transports guests to Mont Tremblant's peak, where they may enjoy amazing views of the surrounding mountains and lakes.

9. Adventure Activities and Ziplining: There are many adventure parks and ziplining activities in the region for adrenaline seekers.

10. Ironman Mont Tremblant: Mont Tremblant hosts the Ironman triathlon event every year, bringing participants from all over the globe for a demanding and spectacular race.

11. Festivals & Events: Mont Tremblant organises a variety of festivals and events throughout the year, including music concerts, cuisine festivals, and cultural festivities.

12. Wellness and spas: Visitors looking to unwind may partake in spa treatments and wellness activities provided by the resort and surrounding businesses.

Mont Tremblant's natural beauty, four-season recreational opportunities, and bustling town environment make it a popular destination for outdoor enthusiasts as well as those looking for a tranquil escape. Whether you prefer winter sports, hiking, or just taking in the alpine scenery, Mont Tremblant provides an unforgettable experience for visitors of all ages and interests.

Thousand Islands

The Thousand Islands are a stunningly gorgeous location between the United States and Canada where the St. Lawrence River meets Lake Ontario. The region is well-known for its beautiful natural landscapes, attractive islands, and a rich history that has drawn people for years. Here are some of the Thousand Islands' main features and attractions:

1. Scenic Cruises: A picturesque boat ride is one of the greatest ways to experience the Thousand Islands. Several tour companies provide cruises that pass by the islands, enabling guests to appreciate the stunning landscape, historic sites, and luxury cottages along the river.

2. Boldt Castle: Boldt Castle, located on Heart Island, is a well-known site in the Thousand Islands. Millionaire George C. Boldt erected the castle in the early 1900s as a memorial to his loving wife. Visitors are welcome to see the castle and gardens and learn about its intriguing history.

3. Alexandria Bay: This beautiful town on the American side of the river is a popular starting point for exploring the Thousand Islands. Visitors

may stroll around the town's shops and eateries, as well as enjoy the gorgeous riverbank.

4. Thousand Islands National Park: Thousand Islands National Park on the Canadian side provides a variety of outdoor activities such as hiking, camping, and kayaking.

5. Boldt Yacht House: The Boldt Yacht House, located next to Boldt Castle, is an outstanding boat house with vintage wooden boats on show.

6. Clayton: On the American side, this lovely town is noted for its bustling arts scene, boutique stores, and museums, notably the Antique Boat Museum.

7. Singer Castle: Singer Castle, located on Dark Island, is a one-of-a-kind attraction with hidden corridors and a rich history. Visitors may explore the castle and its gardens on guided excursions.

8. Zavikon Island: Popular among photographers for its "Zavikon Island Bridge," a narrow bridge linking two small islands.

9. Gananoque: On the Canadian side, Gananoque is known as the "Gateway to the Thousand Islands"

and provides a choice of cruises, shopping, and eating options.

10. Wellesley Island State Park: This state park on the American side offers camping, hiking, and the opportunity to take in the natural splendour of the Thousand Islands.

11. Rock Island Lighthouse State Park: This state park on the American side has a historic lighthouse and magnificent river vistas.

12. Water activities and Fishing: The Thousand Islands area attracts outdoor enthusiasts from all over the globe with chances for boating, fishing, paddleboarding, and other water activities.

The Thousand Islands is a haven for nature lovers, history buffs, and people looking for a peaceful retreat. This scenic location guarantees a wonderful and enchanting experience for those who come, whether you explore by boat, see ancient monuments, or enjoy outdoor activities.

Gatineau

Gatineau is a city in Quebec, Canada, right across the Ottawa River from Ottawa, the country's capital. The two cities are part of the National Capital Region, a thriving metropolitan region. Gatineau is a popular destination for both inhabitants and tourists due to its unique combination of natural beauty, cultural attractions, and outdoor activities. Here are some of Gatineau's main features and attractions:

1. Gatineau Park: One of the city's most distinctive features, Gatineau Park is a vast and beautiful green landscape with hiking and biking trails, scenic lookouts, lakes for swimming and paddling, and cross-country skiing and snowshoeing in the winter. It is a haven for nature aficionados and outdoor enthusiasts.

2. Canadian Museum of History: This remarkable museum, located near the Ottawa River, celebrates Canada's rich history and different cultures via exhibitions, artefacts, and interactive displays.

3. Lac-Leamy Casino: This world-class casino provides gambling, live entertainment, restaurants, and bars to tourists, creating a vibrant and exciting environment.

4. Gatineau Park: This riverside urban park has green spaces, picnic sites, and walking routes, making it a popular destination for leisurely strolls and relaxation.

5. Nordik Spa-Nature: This is North America's biggest spa, with a variety of thermal baths, saunas, and relaxation spaces located in a tranquil natural environment.

6. MosaiCanada 150: A spectacular horticultural show honouring Canada's 150th anniversary, with amazing plant sculptures and lovely landscapes.

7. ByWard Market: The dynamic ByWard Market, situated in Ottawa, is readily accessible from Gatineau and provides a diverse range of stores, restaurants, and a lively ambiance.

8. Gatineau's Maison de la Culture: This cultural centre organises a wide range of creative and cultural activities, including as exhibits, theatrical performances, and concerts.

9. Gatineau's Promenades: This shopping centre is a major retail attraction in the area, with a variety of retailers, restaurants, and entertainment opportunities.

10: Jacques Cartier Park: This park, located along the river, holds a variety of events and festivals throughout the year, making it a cultural and recreational centre.

11. Golf Courses: Gatineau has various golf courses where players may enjoy a game of golf while surrounded by gorgeous scenery.

12. Winterlude: Winterlude, a major winter event including ice sculptures, skating, and other winter sports, is held in Gatineau and Ottawa throughout the winter.

Gatineau is a popular tourist destination because of its natural beauty, cultural attractions, and recreational options. Gatineau offers something for everyone, whether you want to explore the great outdoors, learn about Canadian history and culture, or just enjoy a dynamic city vibe.

Almonte and Mississippi Mills

Almonte is a picturesque town in the municipality of Mississippi Mills in the province of Eastern Ontario, Canada. Almonte and Mississippi Mills, located along the scenic Mississippi River, provide a unique combination of history, culture, and natural beauty. Here are some of the most important features and attractions in Almonte and Mississippi Mills:

1. Almonte's Historic Downtown: Almonte's centre is well-known for its historic architecture, boutique stores, art galleries, and cosy cafés. It's a charming area to wander, shop, and take in the small-town atmosphere.

2. Mill Street: Mill Street, in particular, is a popular tourist destination in Almonte, with its historic buildings and glimpses into the town's industrial history.

3. Almonte Farmers' Market: During the summer months, the local farmers' market provides fresh vegetables, handcrafted items, and an opportunity to engage with the community.

4. Mississippi Riverwalk: The Mississippi Riverwalk is a gorgeous riverfront route that offers a tranquil backdrop for a leisurely stroll or picnic.

5. Almonte Puppets: The town is well-known for its strong puppetry legacy, and Almonte Puppets is a well-known puppet theatre that hosts plays and workshops for people of all ages.

6. Gemmill Park: Gemmill Park in Almonte is a nice green park with a playground, picnic spots, and a splash pad for families to enjoy.

7. Conservation Area of Mill of Kintail: This conservation area, located just outside of Almonte, has excellent hiking paths, waterfalls, and the old Mill of Kintail.

8. Festivals of Maple Syrup: Mississippi Mills conducts yearly Maple Syrup Festivals, which include activities, demonstrations, and delectable sweets to commemorate the region's maple syrup industry.

9. Mississippi Valley Textile Museum: This museum celebrates the region's rich textile legacy with displays on textile arts and history.

10. Stewart Community Centre: For locals and guests, this community centre organises a variety of events, seminars, and recreational activities.

11. Canadian Clock Museum This fascinating museum, located in adjacent Pakenham, has a large collection of clocks and timekeeping gadgets.

12. Ramsayville Bridge: This ancient covered bridge in Ramsayville, near Almonte, is a wonderful site for photography and a reminder of the region's past.

Almonte and Mississippi Mills are ideal for people looking for a relaxing and charming getaway. The area provides a wonderful experience for tourists of all ages with its historic landmarks, natural attractions, and active arts sector. Whether you want to explore the historic downtown, enjoy outdoor activities, or learn about local culture, Almonte and Mississippi Mills have a lot to offer.

SUSTAINABLE TRAVEL IN OTTAWA

Eco-Friendly Accommodations

Choosing eco-friendly lodging is an excellent approach to travel ethically while minimising your environmental effect. Many hotels, lodges, and resorts throughout the globe are now promoting sustainability and conservation by implementing eco-friendly practices. Here are some examples of environmentally friendly lodging:

1. Eco-Friendly Hotels: Many hotels have adopted environmentally friendly practices such as energy-efficient lighting, water-saving fixtures, recycling programmes, and environmentally friendly cleaning solutions. Green accreditation from organisations such as LEED (Leadership in Energy and Environmental Design) or Green Key is also available for certain hotels.

2. Eco-Lodges: Eco-lodges are lodgings that are especially built to have a low environmental effect. They are often constructed using environmentally friendly materials, run on renewable energy, and benefit local communities.

3. Eco-Friendly Resorts: Some luxury resorts have included environmentally responsible practices such as utilising renewable energy, saving water, and supporting local conservation efforts.

4. Nature Retreats and Ecolodges: These accommodations are often found in natural settings such as rainforests, jungles, or national parks and are meant to fit in with the surroundings. They often provide nature-based activities and contribute to conservation initiatives.

5. Green Bed and Breakfasts: Many B&Bs are increasingly integrating environmentally friendly practices such as serving organic and locally produced food, offering recyclable or biodegradable utilities, and installing energy-saving measures.

6. Environmentally Friendly Hostels: Some hostels are adopting environmentally friendly practices including utilising energy-efficient equipment, encouraging visitors to reuse towels and linens, and supporting sustainable tourism projects.

7. Farm Stays: Farm stays provide visitors with a one-of-a-kind eco-friendly experience by allowing them to stay on working farms and learn about

sustainable agriculture and organic farming practices.

8. Glamping Locations: Glamping (glamorous camping) destinations often provide beautiful lodgings in the middle of nature while sticking to eco-friendly ideals such as solar electricity and low-impact infrastructure.

9. Eco-Cabins and Treehouses: Treehouse lodgings and eco-cabins designed with sustainable materials provide a one-of-a-kind and environmentally responsible hotel experience.

10. Community-Based Tourism: Some community-based tourism programmes include homestays or guesthouses maintained by local communities, guaranteeing that tourism benefits local people directly and contributes to their long-term development.

11. Wildlife Conservation Organisations: Wildlife conservancies in certain areas provide lodging alternatives that promote wildlife conservation initiatives and sustainable tourism practices.

When making a reservation, seek for properties that have recognised eco-certifications or green programmes. To make your vacation more ecologically friendly, consider patronising businesses that prioritise sustainability, environmental protection, and responsible tourism practices.

Green Transportation Options

Green transit is critical for lowering your carbon footprint and supporting sustainable travel. There are various eco-friendly transportation options for moving about locally and when travelling. Consider the following green transportation options:

1. Transportation via Public: Taking buses, trains, trams, and subways is one of the most environmentally beneficial methods to get around cities and metropolitan regions. The use of public transport decreases the number of automobiles on the road, resulting in reduced emissions and less traffic congestion.

2. Cycling: Cycling is not only ecologically beneficial, but it is also a terrific method to get a close look at a city or picturesque location. Many cities have designated bike lanes and bike-sharing programmes that make it simple to borrow bicycles for short rides.

3. Walking: The most ecologically friendly way of transportation is walking. It produces no emissions and is a fantastic way to learn about the local culture, scenery, and places.

4. Electric Vehicles (EVs): Because of their zero-emission status, electric automobiles and motorcycles are becoming more popular. Using an electric vehicle, assuming you have access to charging stations, may dramatically lower your carbon footprint when compared to typical gasoline-powered automobiles.

5. Hybrid Vehicles: When compared to traditional vehicles, hybrid vehicles combine an electric motor with a petrol engine, resulting in greater fuel economy and reduced emissions.

6. Ride-Sharing and Carpooling: Sharing transportation decreases the number of automobiles on the road and cuts pollution. Ride-sharing services link drivers and riders who are travelling in the same direction in many cities.

7. High-Speed Rail and Trains: Taking trains or high-speed rail for longer travels saves fuel and emits less emissions than flying or driving.

8. Water Taxis and Ferries: Ferries and water taxis offer a greener option for commuting and tourism in coastal locations and towns with rivers.

9. Environmentally Friendly Car Rentals: For ecologically aware travellers, certain automobile rental businesses now offer hybrid or electric cars.

10. Environmentally Friendly Air Travel: If you must fly, choose airlines with strong environmental commitments and carbon offset programmes to reduce your effect.

11. Green Travel Apps: Use green travel apps to identify eco-friendly transportation alternatives and make more sustainable choices when travelling.

Remember that minimising your trip distance and picking greener solutions wherever feasible may help the environment. You may contribute to a more sustainable and eco-friendly manner of travelling by making thoughtful judgements regarding your transportation options.

Responsible Travel Tips

Responsible travel, often known as sustainable or eco-friendly travel, is making deliberate decisions to reduce your environmental effect, help local people, and protect cultural and natural resources. Here are some ethical and conscious travel guidelines to help you become a more aware and ethical traveller:

1. Respect Local Culture: Learn about the destination's customs, traditions, and manners. Dress properly, respect local customs, and always get permission before photographing people.

2. Promote the Local Economy: Stay at locally owned hotels, dine at local restaurants, and buy gifts from local craftsmen and companies. Your spending has the potential to have a beneficial economic influence on the town.

3. Avoid Single-Use Plastic Bottles: Bring a reusable water bottle and refill it to avoid purchasing single-use plastic bottles. To decrease plastic waste, bring a reusable shopping bag with you when you go shopping.

4. Energy and water conservation: When you leave your accommodation, turn off the lights, air

conditioning, and heating. Take brief showers and be aware of water consumption, particularly in water-stressed places.

5. Select Green Accommodations: Look for eco-friendly hotels, lodges, or resorts that use sustainable practices such as renewable energy, recycling, and water conservation.

6. Walk or use public transportation: To decrease carbon emissions from private automobiles, use public transit, cycling, or walking wherever feasible.

7. Contribute to Conservation Efforts: Visit national parks and animal reserves where conservation and sustainable tourism are prioritised. Respect nature and keep a safe distance from animals.

8. Leave No Trace: Follow the "Leave No Trace" guidelines by cleaning up after oneself and not leaving any trash or rubbish behind. Trash should be disposed of appropriately, and recyclables should be used wherever possible.

9. Reduce Your Carbon Footprint: If you must fly, search for nonstop flights and airlines with carbon offset programmes to pay for your emissions.

10. Practise Responsible Wildlife Tourism: Avoid activities that exploit or hurt wildlife. Select ethical wildlife encounters that put animal care and conservation first.

11. Discover Responsible Wildlife Tourism: Learn about responsible wildlife tourism practices and how to spot and prevent unethical animal encounters.

12. Protect the Environment: Stick to well-marked pathways, avoid harming plants and animals, and never select or gather mementos from natural areas.

13. Be a Responsible Volunteer: If you want to volunteer overseas, be sure that your actions are in line with local requirements and cultural norms. Collaborate with trustworthy organisations that value responsible volunteering.

14. Watch Your Water Use: In locations where water resources are scarce, be very mindful of water usage and avoid wasting water.

By following these responsible travel guidelines, you can have a good influence on the areas you visit, promote sustainable tourism, and contribute to the well-being of local people and the environment. Remember that responsible travel is making informed decisions that respect and preserve the locations for future generations to enjoy.

PRACTICAL INFORMATION

Emergency Contacts

Emergency contacts are important to have when travelling since they allow rapid access to key services in the event of an emergency. Here are some crucial emergency contact numbers to have on hand:

1. Emergency Services in Your Community: Each nation has its own emergency number for police, fire, and medical aid. It's 911 in the United States and Canada. Before travelling to foreign countries, verify the local emergency number.

2. Consulate or Embassy: Find your native country's closest embassy or consulate. They can help you with legal matters, misplaced passports, and crises affecting nationals of your country.

3. Emergency Medical Services: Investigate local hospitals, clinics, and medical centres in the region you want to visit. Maintain easy access to their contact information.

4. Travel Insurance Provider: Carry your travel insurance provider's contact information and policy

details with you. They can help you with medical situations, vacation cancellations, and misplaced luggage.

5. Family and Friends: Maintain a list of emergency contact information for family members or friends who should be alerted in the event of an emergency.

6. Municipal Police Station: Take down the phone number for the local police station in the region where you are staying.

7. Poison Control Centre: In certain nations, the poison control centre has its own phone number. This number must be memorised in case of accidental poisoning.

8. Roadside help: If you intend to hire a vehicle, have the rental car company's roadside help contact information on hand.

9. Airlines or Travel Companies: Keep contact information for individual travel providers, such as airlines, tour operators, or housing hosts, in case of travel cancellations or delays.

10. Medical and Allergy Information: Carry information about any allergies or medical issues,

as well as any essential medicines, if you have them. You might also wear a medical alert bracelet or necklace.

11. Credit Cards Lost or Stolen: Keep your credit card providers' contact information on hand in case your cards are lost or stolen.

12. Translation of Local Emergency Services: If you are travelling in a foreign country and do not know the local language, consider carrying a translation card with local emergency numbers and vital medical information.

Keep these emergency contact numbers on your phone, on a piece of paper, or in your wallet. It's always preferable to be prepared for the unexpected while travelling, and having these contacts on hand may make a big difference in an emergency.

Money-Saving Tips

Saving money when travelling allows you to stretch your budget and experience more throughout your vacation. Here are some money-saving travel tips:

1. plan a Budget: Prior to your vacation, plan and adhere to a budget. Make a budget for lodging,

transportation, food, activities, and mementos. A well-defined budget can assist you in prioritising your spending and avoiding needless costs.

2. Travel Off-Peak Seasons: Travelling during off-seasons or shoulder seasons may frequently result in considerable discounts on flights, lodging, and tourist attractions. Prices are usually cheaper, and there are less people.

3. Make use of fare comparison websites: Use ticket comparison services to obtain the cheapest airfare rates when purchasing flights. If possible, be flexible with your trip dates, since flights on certain days of the week might be cheaper.

4. Select Low-Cost Accommodation: To save money on lodging, consider staying in hostels, guesthouses, or cheap hotels. Many hostels include individual rooms, which may be less expensive than hotels.

5. Cook Your Meals: If your lodging has a kitchen, try preparing part of your meals. Local markets and food shops might be less expensive than dining out every meal.

6. Look for activities that are free or low-cost: On your trip, look for free or low-cost activities and attractions. Many cities have free walking tours, free entrance days to museums, and parks where you may enjoy nature without paying money.

7. Take Public Transportation or Walk: Instead of utilising cabs or private transfers, walk or use public transit throughout the city. It is typically less expensive and enables you to immerse yourself in the local culture.

8. Avoiding Currency Exchange Fees: To avoid excessive currency conversion costs, use credit cards with no international transaction fees or a travel-friendly debit card. To avoid unnecessary fees, utilise ATMs associated with local banks.

9. Make a Reservation in Advance: Booking flights, lodging, and activities ahead of time may frequently result in better bargains and discounts.

10. Seek out Travel Deals and Promotions: Stay up to speed on discounts and special deals by subscribing to travel deal websites, newsletters, and social media profiles.

11. Pack lightly to avoid checked luggage costs on flights. Having fewer baggage also makes it simpler to take public transit and stroll to your destination.

12. Make use of Travel Reward Points: Use your travel reward points or credit card miles to offset travel costs or to gain discounts on flights and hotels.

13. Price Negotiation: Bargaining is a prevalent practice in various nations, particularly in marketplaces and small stores. Don't be scared to bargain for souvenirs or local services.

You may save money when travelling without sacrificing experiences or happiness by being careful of your spending and making wise decisions. Remember that tiny savings may pile up over time, enabling you to maximise your vacation opportunities.

Local Customs and Etiquette

Understanding and respecting local traditions and etiquette is important for travellers who want to have a good and culturally sensitive experience in a new place. Because each culture has its own set of norms and traditions, it's essential to adapt to and follow the following local customs and etiquette:

1. Greetings: Learn how to greet locals properly. A handshake is typical in certain cultures, whereas a bow, a kiss on the cheek, or a mere nod may do in others.

2. Dress Code: When visiting religious places or conservative regions, dress modestly and respectfully. Wearing exposing or improper attire is considered insulting in several cultures.

3. Language: Learn the basics of the local language, such as "hello," "thank you," and "please." This demonstrates respect and may go a long way towards making a favourable impression.

4. Table Etiquette: Learn about local table etiquette, such as how to use chopsticks, how to pass plates, and if eating with your hands is allowed.

5. Present-Giving: It is usual in certain cultures to offer a modest gift while visiting someone's house. Be aware of the right sorts of presents to give and when to give them.

6. Tipping: Research local tipping customs. Tipping is not required in certain nations, while it is in others and is considered unfriendly if not given.

7. Personal Space: Respect personal space limits and prevent potentially unwanted physical contact.

8. Photography: Always get permission before photographing individuals, particularly in more conservative societies. Some venues, such as religious sites, may have photography prohibitions.

9. Recognise and Respect Customs: Be receptive of local traditions, even if they contradict your own views or practises.

10. Recognise Cultural Sensitivities: Be mindful of cultural sensitivities in areas such as religion, politics, and social concerns. Make no inappropriate comments or jokes.

11. Queuing and Waiting: Be respectful of lines and lineups in public areas such as train stations or ticket booths.

12. Research Cultural Taboos: Learn about cultural taboos and avoid acts or gestures that may be objectionable in the local culture.

185

13. Accept Invitations Gracefully: If you are invited to someone's house or a neighbourhood event, accept with appreciation and genuine interest in the experience.

14. Use Polite Language and Gestures: Always use polite language and gestures, such as saying "please" and "thank you."

You may develop pleasant encounters with locals and demonstrate that you understand and accept their culture by being courteous and aware of local traditions and etiquette. This will not only improve your travel experience, but it will also foster a more meaningful and unforgettable relationship with the individuals you encounter along the way.

7-Days ITINERARY

Day 1: Getting to Know Ottawa's Charms

Welcome to Ottawa, Canada's gorgeous capital city! Your first day in this ancient and dynamic city will be a lovely combination of culture, history, and natural beauty. Prepare to go on a journey that will take you to the heart of Canada's capital.

Morning: - Begin your day with a hearty breakfast in a cosy neighbourhood café. Enjoy some traditional Canadian fare such as maple syrup pancakes or a classic Canadian bacon breakfast sandwich.

- After breakfast, visit Parliament Hill, Ottawa's renowned emblem. Join a guided tour of the Parliament Buildings to learn about Canada's political history and, if possible, experience the Changing of the Guard event.

- Take a short stroll to the neighbouring Peace Tower for stunning views of the city and the Ottawa River.

Midday: - For lunch, visit the bustling ByWard Market, Canada's oldest public market. With a vast assortment of food sellers and restaurants, you'll be able to satiate your taste buds with a wide choice of world cuisines.

- After lunch, visit the National Gallery of Canada, which houses a magnificent collection of Canadian and international art, including works by well-known painters such as the Group of Seven.

Afternoon: - Take a walk or ride your bike along the gorgeous Rideau Canal, a UNESCO World Heritage Site that runs through the centre of the city. During the summer, you may take a leisurely boat ride along the canal.

- Continue your day by visiting the Canadian Museum of History in Gatineau, Quebec, which is just over the river. Investigate the displays that highlight Canada's rich history and cultural heritage.

Evening: Return to Ottawa and have a delicious meal at Elgin Street or the ByWard Market. Ottawa's culinary scene has a wide range of cuisines from throughout the globe, so you may savour traditional Canadian fare or try something new.

- After supper, take a walk over the Alexandra Bridge, which crosses the Ottawa River. This lovely promenade provides breathtaking views of the Parliament Buildings lit against the night sky.

- Finish your day by returning to Parliament Hill to see the magnificent Sound and Light Show, a stunning visual show that chronicles the tale of Canada's history.

You'll fall in love with Ottawa's distinct charm after a day full of historic sites, cultural events, and wonderful food. Get a good night's sleep since there's still so much to see and do in the days ahead!

Day 2: Discovering the Natural Beauty of Ottawa

The schedule for today will take you on a tour to discover Ottawa's spectacular natural landscapes and tranquil outdoor places. Day 2 offers a day of leisure and absorption in nature, with everything from stunning parks to scenic rivers.

Morning: - Begin your day with a full breakfast at a nearby café. Get ready for an eventful day!

- Visit Gatineau Park, which is just a short drive from downtown Ottawa. This enormous natural playground provides plenty of outdoor activities. You may go hiking, riding, or just take a tranquil stroll among the lush woods and picturesque panoramas depending on the season.

- For the more daring, walk to the top of the Champlain Lookout or the Eardley Escarpment. You'll be rewarded with stunning views of the Ottawa Valley and the Gatineau Hills from these vantage points.

Midday: - Take a picnic lunch in Gatineau Park, surrounded by nature's serenity. You may also return to the ByWard Market for a quick meal at one of the market's numerous restaurants.

- After lunch, go to Major's Hill Park, which is near Parliament Hill. This pleasant urban park is a great place to unwind and admire the splendour of the city skyline and the Ottawa River.

Afternoon: - Take a relaxing boat ride along the Rideau Canal, often known as the "Rideau Waterway." This historic canal is one of Ottawa's most beloved sights, and a boat offers a unique viewpoint on the city's waterways and lovely neighbourhoods.

- Alternatively, you may hire a bike and explore the canal's gorgeous riding routes. Make a point of stopping to photograph the stunning locks and scenic bridges along the trip.

Evening: Attend a live performance or play at one of Ottawa's theatres or performing venues for a cultural experience. The city offers a strong cultural culture that includes a wide range of music, dance, and theatre acts.

- Finish your day with a relaxed meal at a restaurant with a view of the Ottawa River. While you dine, you can watch the sunset paint the sky with orange and pink colours, creating a magnificent environment.

- To round up your day of seeing Ottawa's natural splendour, take a leisurely walk along the riverside paths or take a relaxing night time river cruise.

You'll have found the city's synergy with nature and experienced the calm and tranquillity that Ottawa has to offer by the end of Day 2. Tomorrow, as you continue your remarkable adventure through

Canada's capital, prepare to delve further into the city's culture and history.

Day 3: Uncovering Ottawa's Cultural Treasures

On Day 3, we'll dig further into Ottawa's cultural gems, visiting museums, art galleries, and historical places. Prepare for an enlightening day full with fascinating experiences and a greater grasp of Canada's varied past.

Morning: - Begin your day by visiting the Canadian Museum of Nature. This magnificent museum includes a broad variety of exhibits displaying Canada's and the world's natural beauties. The marvels of our world will fascinate you, from dinosaur fossils to beautiful jewels.

- Next, visit the National Arts Centre, Ottawa's performing arts powerhouse. Check their calendar for matinée performances of theatre, dance or musical concerts. Immerse yourself in the cultural arts scene and see the creativity of Canadian artists.

Midday: - For lunch, visit the fashionable and creative Westboro neighbourhood. This lively neighbourhood is filled with attractive boutiques, artisanal stores, and a variety of cafes serving a wide range of cuisines. Relax with a leisurely meal at one of the nearby cafés or bistros.

- After lunch, travel to Gatineau, Quebec, to see the Canadian Museum of History (previously the Canadian Museum of Civilization). Investigate the intriguing exhibitions that tell the narrative of Canada's rich cultural heritage and indigenous history.

Afternoon: - Continue your investigation of the Canadian Museum of History, where you may learn about Canada's many cultures and customs.

- If you like art, go visit the National Gallery of Canada for a fascinating voyage through the worlds of Canadian and worldwide art. Discover treasures by well-known painters, such as works by the Group of Seven and Indigenous art from around Canada.

Evening: For supper, return to the ByWard Market neighbourhood, where you'll discover a variety of restaurants serving a variety of cuisines to suit your taste. Whether you're craving French cuisine, seafood, or fusion meals, the market provides something for everyone.

- After supper, meander along the Rideau Canal or pay a visit to the magnificent Château Laurier, a famous hotel that emanates elegance and history. The surrounding region provides stunning views of Parliament Hill, particularly when lighted at night.

- Finish your day by taking in Ottawa's lively nightlife. Explore bustling bars and cosy pubs, or enjoy a live music performance at a neighbourhood establishment. Engage with the inhabitants and immerse yourself in the inviting environment of the city.

By the end of Day 3, you'll have a better understanding of Canada's cultural legacy and artistic accomplishments. We'll continue our tour across Ottawa tomorrow, discovering more hidden treasures and enjoying the city's distinct character. Prepare for another exciting day of exploration!

Day 4: Historical Highlights and Local Delights in Ottawa

On Day 4, we'll explore Ottawa's historical sights and landmarks, transporting you to the city's history and present. This day offers a combination of cultural and gastronomic pleasures, from ancient structures to local treats.

Morning: - Begin your day by visiting the Canadian War Museum. This intriguing museum depicts Canada's military history, from World War I to modern wars. It serves as a moving reminder of the sacrifices made by Canadian troops.

- Next, go to adjacent LeBreton Flats to see the Canadian Museum of History's major display, the Canadian History Hall. This interactive experience traces Canada's history from Indigenous civilizations to present times.

- For a change of pace, visit Merrickville, a charming community just outside of Ottawa. Merrickville, known for its well-preserved 19th-century buildings and artisanal businesses, provides a beautiful insight into the past.

Midday: Have a leisurely lunch at one of Merrickville's quaint cafés or diners. Enjoy regional specialties while taking in the small-town atmosphere.

- Return to Ottawa after lunch for a walk through the scenic Sparks strip Mall, a pedestrian strip dotted with stores, restaurants, and lively street acts.

Afternoon: - Discover the rich history of the Rideau Canal, a UNESCO World Heritage Site. Visit the Bytown Museum near the Rideau Canal's Ottawa Locks to learn about the canal's construction and its significance in determining the city's growth.

- Visit Rideau Hall, the main house of Canada's Governor General. Stroll around the lovely grounds and see the antique architecture of this important national icon.

Evening: Return to the ByWard Market for a delectable supper experience. You may select from a variety of eating alternatives, including foreign cuisine and Canadian favourites.

- For dessert, try the classic "Beavertails"—a delightful Canadian confection fashioned like a beaver's tail and commonly covered with sweet toppings like cinnamon and sugar.

- Consider taking a sunset sail along the Ottawa River after supper. Witness the city's monuments bathed in the golden light of the setting sun, providing a spectacular spectacle that will last a lifetime.

- Alternatively, spend the evening in one of Ottawa's thriving entertainment districts, which include live music venues, theatres, and thrilling nightlife.

By the end of Day 4, you'll have learned about Ottawa's rich history and sampled some of its unique delicacies. Prepare for further exploration tomorrow as we journey into Ottawa's varied neighbourhoods to discover its distinct offers. Prepare for another day of exploration and fun in Canada's capital

Day 5: Neighbourhoods and Culinary Delights in Ottawa

Day 5 will take you through Ottawa's lively neighbourhoods, each with their own unique personality and charm. Prepare to explore vibrant streets and indulge in scrumptious culinary delights as you experience the city like a resident.

Morning: - Begin your day with a relaxing breakfast at a small café in the fashionable Hintonburg neighbourhood. This artistic neighbourhood is well-known for its creative population and varied mix of businesses.

- After breakfast, meander along Wellington Street West, which is dotted with shops, art galleries, and delightful restaurants. Discover one-of-a-kind handmade goods, art pieces, and mementos that represent the neighbourhood's inventiveness.

- Don't miss the Ottawa Farmers' Market in Lansdowne Park on weekends. Immerse yourself in a dynamic environment brimming with fresh vegetables, artisanal goods, and local crafts.

Midday: - For lunch, visit the historic Glebe neighbourhood, which is home to a varied range of eateries serving foreign cuisines. Whether you're seeking sushi, Mediterranean dining, or traditional pub meal, the Glebe offers something for everyone.

- After lunch, meander through the Glebe's lush alleys dotted with attractive historical houses before heading to Patterson Creek Park for a pleasant afternoon stroll.

Afternoon: - Explore Ottawa's Chinatown, which is situated just west of downtown. Walk along Somerset Street West, which is lined with Chinese restaurants, bakeries and specialised businesses.

- Treat yourself to a scrumptious afternoon tea at one of Ottawa's exquisite tearooms. In a classy atmosphere, savour exquisite pastries, finger sandwiches, and a selection of tea blends.

- Continue your day to the Ottawa work Gallery, which features modern and traditional work by local and Canadian artists. Explore the intriguing exhibitions and obtain a better understanding of Ottawa's creative community.

Evening: - For supper, go to Little Italy, where you may dine at a cosy trattoria or a family-owned pizza. Enjoy traditional Italian cuisine while taking in the warm and friendly ambiance.

- After supper, stroll through the lovely alleys of Old Ottawa South, a relaxed neighbourhood filled with shops, bookstores, and cosy cafés. This neighbourhood is ideal for an evening walk or a relaxed drink at a local pub.

- Cap off your day with a drink at one of Ottawa's artisan brewers or speakeasy-style pubs. Try locally made beers or inventive cocktails created by expert mixologists.

By the end of Day 5, you'll have explored Ottawa's many neighbourhoods and savoured its gastronomic pleasures. We'll go farther out tomorrow to experience Ottawa's natural beauties and neighbouring attractions. Prepare for another day of exploration and fun in Canada's vibrant capital city!!

Day 6: Surrounding Wonders & Nearby Attractions in Ottawa

On Day 6, we'll leave the city boundaries to see Ottawa's natural beauties and adjacent attractions. This day promises to be full of excitement and adventure, with everything from magnificent natural scenery to historical places.

Morning: - Begin your day with an early trip to Wakefield, a lovely community only a short drive from Ottawa. Wakefield, located along the Gatineau River, has a charming and creative atmosphere.

- Stroll through the lovely village's tiny alleyways dotted with artisanal stores, galleries, and cosy cafés. Don't pass up the chance to enjoy a delicious breakfast at one of the neighbourhood restaurants.

- After breakfast, return to Gatineau Park to partake in additional outdoor activities. Consider going on a leisurely walk or bike ride to discover new pathways and take in the natural beauty of the park.

Midday: - For lunch, treat yourself to a farm-tothetable eating experience at one of Wakefield's quaint eateries. Many restaurants in the neighbourhood take pleasure in utilising fresh, locally produced food.

- After lunch, go to the well-known Wakefield Covered Bridge, a lovely landmark that is great for photography and a leisurely stroll along the river.

Afternoon: Return to Ottawa and see the intriguing Canadian Museum of Immigration at Pier 21. This museum tells the experiences of immigrants who came to Canada through Pier 21 in Halifax, giving visitors a better appreciation of the country's multicultural fabric.

- Visit the Canada Aviation and Space Museum if you're interested in aviation history. Explore the remarkable collection of planes and artefacts that reveals Canada's aviation history.

Evening: For supper, go back to Ottawa's lively city centre or another neighbourhood you haven't seen yet. Choose from the city's numerous culinary choices, which include everything from foreign cuisine to contemporary Canadian food.

- After supper, try attending a performance at the National Arts Centre, where you may see the abilities of world-class musicians, dancers, and theatre companies.

- As the evening draws to a close, take a leisurely stroll down the Rideau Canal to take in the tranquil atmosphere of the city's waterways at night.

By the end of Day 6, you'll have seen the beauty of Ottawa's environs and gotten a better understanding of Canada's history and cultural variety. We'll finish our adventure in Ottawa tomorrow, making the most of our remaining time in this fascinating city. Prepare for a last day of exploring and heartfelt farewells

Day 7: Goodbye and Departure

Day 7 enables you to savour the closing moments of your vacation and say goodbye to this wonderful city as your remarkable experience in Ottawa comes to a close.

Morning: Begin your last day in Ottawa with a leisurely breakfast at your hotel or a nearby café. Take some time to think of the great experiences you've had throughout your stay.

- If you need any last-minute shopping or souvenirs, go to the ByWard Market or other artisanal stores in the city. Find souvenirs to remember you of the great experiences you had in Ottawa.

- Before you leave your hotel, take one final glance at the city skyline and reflect on the memories you've formed throughout your stay.

Midday: Depending on your departure schedule, you may be able to see one last attraction or location that grabbed your attention throughout your vacation. Enjoy these final minutes of discovery by returning to a favourite institution or wandering through a favourite park.

- For lunch, try a new place or go back to one of your old favourites. Savour the local food one final time before saying goodbye to Ottawa's flavours.

Afternoon: As the afternoon draws near, make your way to the airport, railway station, or bus terminal to begin your trip back home or to your next destination. If you have time before your flight, rest in the airport lounge or go through your trip notebook to recall your travels.

- If your schedule permits, try planning a last-minute activity or short trip to maximise your time in the city. Enjoy every moment until it's time to go, whether it's a picturesque boat ride or a visit to a neighbouring destination.

Evening: Take one final look at the city from above as you board your aircraft or train, or say farewell to the kind folks that made your time in Ottawa memorable.

- Take advantage of your journey time to think of the fantastic experiences and fresh views you've obtained throughout your stay in Ottawa.

As you make your way back home, remember that you are leaving Ottawa with fond memories, more knowledge, and the desire to return one day. Your heart has been left indelible by Ottawa's unique

combination of history, culture, and natural beauty.
Farewell and safe travels till the next journey!!

CONCLUSION

Finally, Ottawa, Canada, entices visitors with its charm, history, and natural beauty, making it a must-see destination for visitors from all over the globe. This Ottawa 2023 travel guide was created to be your trusty companion on an amazing trip around this vibrant capital city.

Every step of your tour, from the magnificent Parliament Hill to the scenic Rideau Canal, has been intended to immerse you in Ottawa's unique tapestry of culture and legacy. You've walked through colourful neighbourhoods, savoured wonderful culinary delights, and visited world-class museums and art galleries that highlight the country's inventiveness.

Ottawa's warm and inviting atmosphere has engulfed you during your stay, generating a feeling of belonging in a city that embraces variety and inclusiveness. The encounters you've had, the people you've met, and the sites you've seen have left an indelible mark on your heart and spirit.

In 2023, Ottawa will continue to grow, with new attractions, events, and experiences that will pique your interest and pique your curiosity. Your tour has been a celebration of growth and preservation as the city welcomes the future while honouring its heritage.

Take with you beloved memories and greater information when you flip the last pages of this travel guide. Ottawa's rich history and cultural legacy have shaped your perception of Canada, and its dedication to sustainability has motivated you to travel ethically.

May your experiences in Ottawa remind you of the treasures that await you in every location you visit. The experiences you've made here will remain with you, inspiring new excursions and investigations.

As you say goodbye to Ottawa, remember that the city's spirit, its busy streets, its compelling history, and its kind residents will always welcome you back. Safe travels till we meet again, and may the spirit of Ottawa accompany you on your future trips, wherever they may take you.

Made in the USA
Middletown, DE
08 August 2023

36384009R00116